Popular Bonsai

POPULAR
Bonsai

Dave Pike

The Crowood Press

First published in 1991 by
The Crowood Press Ltd
Ramsbury, Marlborough
Wiltshire
SN8 2HR

British Library Cataloguing in Publication Data

Pike, Dave
 Popular bonsai.
 1. Bonsai
 I. Title
 635.9772

 ISBN 1 85223 3621

Picture Credits
All photographs by Dave Pike, except those on pages 113 (right), 127
and 140, which are reproduced courtesy of G. Owen.
Illustrations by Claire Upsdale-Jones.

Month	Northern hemisphere	Southern hemisphere
	Readers should note that in order to make the text appropriate to both hemispheres the following guide is offered:	
January	Mid-winter	Mid-summer
February	Late winter	Late summer
March	Early spring	Early autumn
April	Mid-spring	Mid-autumn
May	Late spring	Late autumn
June	Early summer	Early winter
July	Mid-summer	Mid-winter
August	Late summer	Late winter
September	Early autumn	Early spring
October	Mid-autumn	Mid-spring
November	Late autumn	Late spring
December	Early winter	Early summer

Typeset by Inforum Typesetting, Portsmouth
Printed and bound by Times Publishing Group, Singapore

CONTENTS

Introduction   7

Part I

1 Beginners' Bonsai   10
2 Soil   30
3 Propagation   42
4 Cuttings for Hardy and Indoor Bonsai   50
5 Pests and Diseases   61
6 Month-by-Month Guide   72
7 Advanced Techniques   82

Part II

8 An A–Z of Hardy Bonsai   110
9 An A–Z of Indoor Bonsai   148

Glossary   173
Index of Tree Names   174
General Index   175

INTRODUCTION

'Bonsai' is the method of cultivating an artifically dwarfed potted plant or small tree. As far as the records show, growing miniature trees in small pots started in China and was mainly connected with religious followings of Taoism, later Buddhism, and one teaching in particular: Zen Buddhism. As the faith spread, so too did the small trees.

Around the twelfth century – or the Japanese *Kamakura* period (1186–1333) – Japan invited Chinese monks to help build Zen Buddhist temples. At the same time Japanese monks were also visiting China and an exchange of architecture and religious philosophy was taking place. This could have initiated the Japanese art we now call bonsai. The keeping of these small trees, however, was mainly restricted to religious temples or the wealthy. Trees were collected from the mountains and usually kept in the style in which they were found. Up to the 1930s in Japan, bonsai trees were surrounded by religious items, but slowly the bonsai started to take its place on its own alongside other forms of art. In time, these small trees became known to the masses and to meet demand from all social levels, trees were commercially trained and shaped through artistic means rather than collected from the wild.

ART AND LIVING PLANTS

It is true to say that bonsai is a form of living

Fig 1   *Ginkgo biloba* – a typical Chinese tree.

art. It is a plant quite normal in its genetic make-up, but sculptured by mechanical processes such as root pruning, selective branch pruning, pinching and wiring, to look like a mature tree similar to those growing in the wild, or a tree which partly resembles a tree shape but to which character has been added. However, even in Japan there are different schools of thought regarding how far

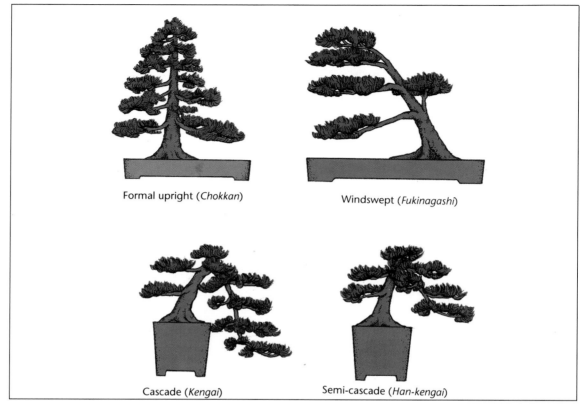

Fig 2   Four different styles of bonsai.

the man-made artistic character should be applied. The modern day bonsai shapes and styles reflect many different ways of growing and as the art of cultivating these small trees expands throughout the world, new styles and shapes will emerge to express the growers' artistic feel for working with nature.

THE TRUE TREE SHAPE

This is when a tree is trained to look like its normal undamaged counterpart found growing in the wild. Most beginners start at this stage and even the advanced student will maintain such a tree. After a year or so,

however, many bonsai students will copy the more authentic Chinese or Japanese styles such as the curving or informal upright (*Moyogi*), cascade (*Kengai*), semi-cascade (*Han-kengai*) or windswept (*Fukinagashi*), shown in Fig 2.

These are slightly removed from the tree shapes found in local parks, by artistically adding characteristics such as branches all facing the same way or trees with a flat top, both caused by the effect of weather and adverse growing. Some will prefer to model their trees on tree shapes found in their own region of the world and, as the Japanese created their own style from a Chinese method, so will other countries continue to add theirs.

Part I

Chapter 1

BEGINNERS' BONSAI

One of the first questions that may spring to your mind is, 'What is the difference between a hardy and an indoor bonsai?' Although the root pruning and training is basically the same for both the hardy and the indoor bonsai, there is a big difference in terms of placement, temperature and light. The reason for the death of so many bonsai kept indoors is that hardy outdoor bonsai are expected to live under houseplant conditions. I would therefore suggest that you read through Chapters 8 and 9 and learn as much as possible about the type of plants (not all of them can be classed as trees), and the growing conditions that produce best results.

HARDY BONSAI

The beginner who chooses to grow hardy rather than indoor bonsai has more to choose from in the way of starting material, such as three types of cuttings instead of two (*see* Chapter 4). Seeds can be collected from the wild or, as suggested in Chapter 3, you may jump both the seed and cutting stages and purchase nursery stock aged one or more years.

However, you should keep to seedlings between the age of one and three years old. I would also advise you to leave the pine tree until you have spent one or two years working on other evergreen trees such as a juniper and deciduous trees.

INDOOR BONSAI

The market for indoor bonsai has grown a great deal in the past five years. Indoor bonsai appeal mainly to the first-time buyer or the buyer purchasing a tree as a gift. This increase in demand has encouraged many commercial growers to grow bonsai and, unfortunately, not always successfully. Many beginners therefore start by buying, or being given, a tree, but in most cases lose it within a few months. In a great number of cases the tree sold is not suited to its eventual environment (including centrally-heated houses and poor light conditions). Therefore, a study of the plant and its ideal growing conditions should be examined before a purchase is made.

Alternatively, you can grow your own bonsai, but unlike the hardy bonsai with its abundance of raw material, the indoor plant matter is harder to find. It is very doubtful whether such a plant suitable for indoor bonsai will be available at your local garden centre, although you may find something in the houseplant section. If not, you will need to find a nursery which specializes in houseplants or visit a bonsai centre to purchase an indoor seedling or a packet of indoor seeds. Finally, you can use cuttings.

Some of the more unusual plant material may have to be ordered from a specialist. If this is the case, then why not order two and use one as a stock plant? A stock plant is not grown as a bonsai, but treated as a normal

Stock Plant
Some of the more unusual plant material may have to be ordered from a specialist. If this is the case, then why not order two and use one as a stock plant? A stock plant is not grown as a bonsai but treated as a normal plant growing in a large pot. It is encouraged to push out new branches, which in turn are used to produce cuttings. Once you have purchased a suitable stock plant for indoor bonsai growing, cuttings such as softwood and semi-ripe can be taken once or twice a year, (*see* Chapter 4).

plant growing in a large pot. It is encouraged to push out new branches which in turn are used to produce cuttings. Once you have purchased a suitable stock plant for indoor bonsai growing, cuttings such as softwood and semi-ripe can be taken once or twice a year (*see* Chapter 4).

Seeds

Once planted, most seeds for the indoor bonsai will need some form of heat for successful germination, as shown in the propagation section in Chapter 3.

The temperature for general seed sowing should be 12–18°C (54–64°F), but some of the exotic trees such as baobab may need a slightly higher temperature (*see* Chapter 9).

Seed Packets
Tropical tree seeds suitable for indoor bonsai can sometimes be ordered through your local garden centre, but in most cases it will be a case of ordering from a seed specialist or bonsai centre.

Cuttings

Cuttings for the hardy bonsai are divided into three types:

1. Softwood, March/April.
2. Semi-ripe, June/July.
3. Hardwood, October/November.

Cuttings for the indoor bonsai are divided into two groups:

1. Softwood, March/April.
2. Semi-ripe, June/July.

Softwood and semi-ripe cuttings, once they have taken root, can be transplanted into individual pots. Hardwood cuttings which have rooted can be directly planted into the ground or into a standard cutting mix (50 per cent sand, 50 per cent moss peat).

FIRST YEAR

From Seed to Cutting

Once the seeds have germinated and the stem is starting to become firm, prick out the seedlings into individual pots. I prefer to use a deeper pot at this stage rather than shallow bonsai one, as the roots need as much space as possible to develop. Care should be taken not to damage the young stem, shoots and roots when removing from the compost. Try to lift the seedling by first taking hold of one of the cotyledons with your finger and thumb (cotyledons are the leaves that develop prior to the leaves proper), then lift the roots very carefully and with as much compost as possible and transplant. Make a hole with a dibber into a compost Code 3 or 4, according to whether the tree likes an acidic or neutral compost. Remember, do not prune the roots at this stage or throughout the first year.

Once you have successfully transplanted them, place the cuttings back into the same, pre-transplanting temperature and growing conditions and leave them in this position for the next week or two.

After this period – once the young cuttings are showing signs of healthy growth – move them closer to the door if grown in a glasshouse; leave the top slightly open if grown in a cold frame for the hardy bonsai or move to a cooler position in the glasshouse or indoor growing area in the case of the indoor bonsai; turn off the power supply and allow more air to enter if grown in a small propagator. This will gradually introduce the cuttings into normal weather or surrounding conditions, will harden them off and avoid 'shocking' them by placing them outside too soon.

Seeds and Cuttings
Keep the temperature between 16–18°C (61–64°F) and give the seedling as much light as possible, or use one of the grow-lite bulbs, but avoid strong sunlight. Turn the seedling over each day to ensure that it receives light from all sides in order to give it a balanced growth pattern and pinch out top growth to encourage a bushy growth. Make sure that the ventilation is adequate to avoid diseases such as mould.

Cutting Aftercare
Check for new growth and a white root system. If the cuttings have rooted, pot as for the softwood cutting.
   For those plants and trees classed as 'cold room' bonsai, such as the olive, and grown in a cold frame with heated cables, allow plenty of ventilation on warm days, but beware of sudden changes in weather conditions. Alternatively, slowly introduce them indoors into well-lit, cold room conditions, avoiding direct sunlight.

heated houses for example; and every other day with other types of heating. If the water level is higher than the drainage hole, this will hinder drainage and stop the flow of air from circulating downwards from the top of the pot and through the drainage hole.

After two weeks, plan a feeding programme (as shown), starting with a foliar feed. The tree will be fed through its leaves, at the same time leaving the root system free to develop its very fine feeding hairs. (Refer to pages 37 and 38 for information on N.P.K.)

Watering and Feeding

Do not feed for the first two weeks after transplanting and never allow the compost to become waterlogged by overwatering or by standing the pot in a tray of water. Water before the compost becomes completely dry, or as a general rule, every other day, or every day during hot weather. Always try to water before 10 o'clock in the morning or after 5 o'clock in the evening to avoid scorching the leaves (the water droplets being magnified by the sun's rays). Mist over the foliage if the atmosphere becomes dry; every day in the case of the indoor bonsai kept under dry conditions, in gas central-

Feeding Programme	
April–May	Foliar feed with an N:7 P:7 K:7 plus trace elements.
June–August	Change to a fertilizer containing N:10 P:14 K:18 plus trace elements.
September (hardy bonsai)	Stop feeding at the end of September.
September–February (indoor bonsai)	Use a tomato feed with trace elements.
March (hardy/indoor bonsai)	Do not feed as this is the root-pruning time.

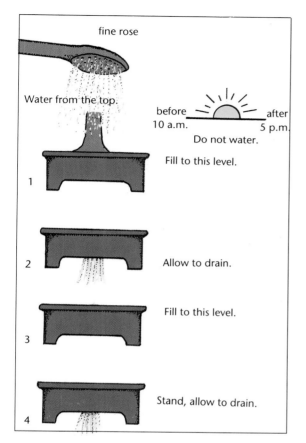

Fig 3   Always water with a fine rose and from the top of the pot.

Training

The training of cuttings is the same for both the hardy and indoor bonsai, except that when hardening off the indoor bonsai, more attention should be given to the temperature factor and the frost problem (*see* Chapter 5 and Chapters 8 and 9 for weather conditions).

Pinching, pruning, bud rubbing and wiring form the basic training for the hardy and indoor bonsai. This training is followed for the next five years and we term it 'cosmetic' training.

Stopping
Pinch out the growing tips during the first year (this will encourage the plant to bush out) but do not attempt to prune the root system at this stage. Remove any unwanted buds to avoid overcrowding and crossing branches.

Pruning
Making a clean cut to avoid leaving stumps will prevent diseases and get rid of areas which insects can use as breeding grounds. The angle of the cut is very important. It should be made to encourage rainwater and moisture in general to run away from the base of the bud or pruned area. This will then avoid the build up of moisture in the base of the bud or in hollows.

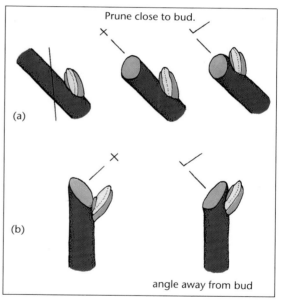

Fig 4   The right and wrong ways of pruning cuts and angles. (a) Be sure to prune close to bud. (b) Prune at an angle to prevent a build-up of water at the base of the bud.

Pruning to a bud   This is the natural way to shape your tree without the aid of wire. It has the advantage of avoiding wire

[13]

marks, but has the disadvantage of producing a formal shape only.

Forming a basic shape from buds can be an easy task, however, if the plant is of the flowering type and the beginner wishes to produce the flowers, then pruning to a bud has to follow a slightly different pattern as shown in Chapter 7. However, you should initially concentrate on a basic shape before attempting to produce flowers. First, select a bud which is facing the direction in which you would like to form a branch. By cutting back to this bud you will force the new growth in that direction as shown in Fig 5 (*see also* renewal pruning, Chapter 7, page 95).

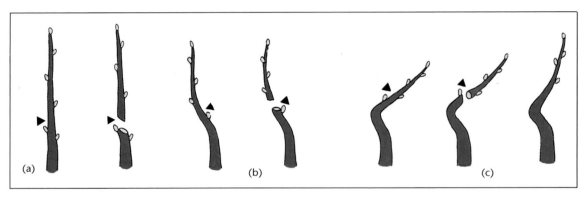

Figs 5(a), (b) and (c)   Pruning to a bud is a natural way of shaping the tree without wiring.

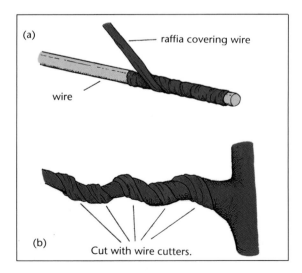

Fig 6   Wiring.   (a) Raffia will help to protect the bark from damage. (b) Never try to remove the wire by unwinding. Using wire cutters, cut at the points shown.

Wiring

Wiring should only be carried out if you are unable to shape the bonsai by pruning and you should not assume that every bonsai should be wired. In fact bonsai wire can be very damaging if it is placed on the trunk or branches too tightly, or if it covers the buds. Therefore I would suggest that you practise on an old piece of wood first.

Do not over-wire your tree during the first year and try to shape from buds as far as possible. If you do have to wire in the first year, make sure the branch is woody (brown or turning brown) and not green or sappy, otherwise the wire will cut and damage the bark, leaving it open and exposed to diseases and sap-sucking insects. For seedlings whose bark damages very easily, cover the wire with raffia. I prefer to cover the wire on all trees during their first two years, but if you use the soft wire now being imported from Japan, this is not necessary.

The wire used for bonsai today is made of aluminium rather than copper and can be purchased in several different gauges, ranging from 1.0 to 6mm. The thicker the trunk, the thicker the wire. In some cases, two different gauges are used, one thick and one thin.

The wire should not be too tightly bound, but at the same time, it should be secure enough to hold the branch or trunk in the position in which it has been set. The anchorage point plays the most important part. If the wire is not anchored, you will find that the wire will start to unravel itself and the shape will not be held.

You should never leave the wire on for more than one growing season. A branch can always be rewired but it is very hard to remove the scar. Many imported trees show

Fig 7 Wire (here, embedded), will leave scars if left on the tree too long.

signs of over-wiring, some even still contain pieces of wire embedded in their bark. If you should purchase such a bonsai, remove the wire as soon as possible or reject the tree if the wire is embedded too deep into the bark. It is very easy to damage branches when removing wire. Cut the wire at specific points (*see* Fig 7) and it will practically fall off without damaging the branch.

Main trunk Bonsai seedlings between one to three years of age lend themselves quite readily to being shaped with wire, but for older bonsai it may be advisable to use a clamp.

For those bonsai with a supple trunk whose bark has started to form a woody texture, start by cutting a length of wire slightly longer than the trunk, then push the wire into the soil as shown in Fig 8(a). Be sure to anchor the wire in a secure manner.

Working upwards, wrap the wire around the trunk, avoiding any buds you may wish to keep, as shown in Fig 8(e). Hold the base of the tree firmly (or have someone hold it for you) to avoid any movement of the root ball, then with great care, and always remembering not to cover any of the buds or break any of the growing points you wish to keep, wrap the wire from the base of the tree up to the top of the tree. Once the wire is secured, bend and twist the trunk until you reach the desired shape as shown in Fig 8(b), (c) and (d).

Branch You can, after practising, wire two branches at the same time with one strand of wire and using the centre or main trunk as an anchoring point.

First, select two branches close to each other as shown in Fig 9. Cut a piece of wire long enough to wire both branches, then, start from the middle of the wire and wire branch (a), then do the same to branch (b).

The most important thing to remember when wiring double or single branches is to

[15]

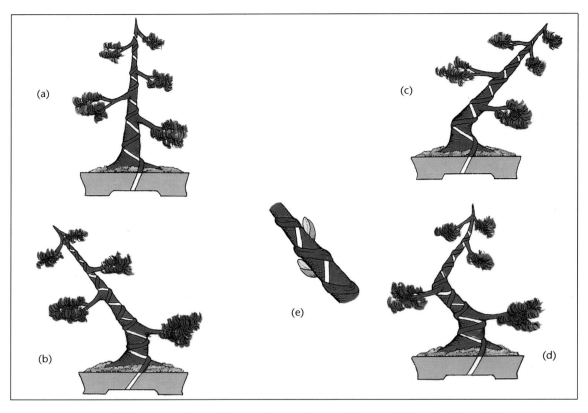

Fig 8   Wiring. (a) Push the wire into the pot then work up to the top of the tree. (b) Bend as shown. (c) Shape the main trunk with wire. (d) Never allow the wire to cut into the trunk. (e) Avoid covering buds.

Wiring
As a general rule, place the wire on the previous season's wood at the beginning of a growing season, just before bud burst and remember, do not wire very young, green or sappy growth.

anchor the middle of the wire first and, as mentioned before, avoid covering any buds you may wish to keep for further development.

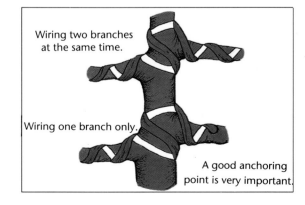

Fig 9   To create a more artistic shape, most trees will have to be wired.

Air-Layering

There are three ways to air-layer which are shown in the section on propagation in Chapter 4.

Grafting

See section on grafting in Chapter 4.

SECOND YEAR

The indoor bonsai is not governed by the same rules as the outdoor hardy one, simply because it has to be kept in warmer conditions and a frost-free growing area. Therefore, with the exception of the flowering period, root pruning and repotting can take place at almost any time of the year. However, this book is written to encourage the beginner to grow both indoor *and* hardy bonsai and therefore it is far better to keep to a root-pruning programme. I prefer to root-prune during the months of March and April because the seed or cutting sown or taken in the previous spring will then be one year old and starting to develop strong healthy growth. Root pruning, however, can take place from September to October.

Records
It is a good idea to keep a yearly record of root-pruning and, likewise, of feeding and spraying. This will ensure that you do not root-prune twice or overfeed.

Pruning Times

Indoor Bonsai

For those of you who will only grow indoor bonsai (which means that the tree will continue to make new growth throughout the year), it would be far better to concentrate on shape and style during the spring and summer months. Lack of light and fluctuations in temperature may induce the tree to slow down during the winter period. However, once your tree has developed large, woody branches, it would be advisable to remove any unwanted, large branches during the winter period. The sap flow is not as active then, and only in the case of an emergency, such as a broken branch or a disease problem, should a large branch be removed during the summer months.

Hardy Bonsai

Most hardy bonsai, except pines and conifers, are deciduous and they therefore only grow from March to October (in some exceptional years, this may be extended or reduced). Pines and conifers show signs of stopping all growth during the winter months, but in fact they only slow down their growth rate. Cosmetic pruning and shaping again only take place during the spring and summer months and is reduced during the autumn until it is stopped completely around the end of September, with the exception of removing large branches during the winter months.

Root Pruning

Remove the tree from its pot. If the tree is pot-bound, you may have to run a knife around the inside of the pot. Then, working from the sides down to the bottom of the root system, loosen one third of the root system as shown.

Cut the loosened part of the root system; at the same time, check for signs of pest and disease. If the root system shows any sign of pest, disease or damage, do not root-prune, but gently wash away the soil and remove pest or, if diseased, spray with a fungicide or remove infected areas by hand. Once you are satisfied that the tree is free from pest or disease, repot it without root pruning back into a clean container with fresh soil.

[17]

Fig 10   Root pruning and repotting. (a) The tree before root pruning. (b) Starting from the sides, loosen one-third of the root system. (c) Remove one-third of the root system with the aid of pruning shears. (d) Place a piece of mesh over the drainage hole, followed by 6mm gravel. (e) Work some fresh soil in between the root system until the pot is filled (f).

Repotting

First, place a piece of mesh over the drainage hole or holes, then cover this with 6mm of washed gravel, which plays a very important part in the drainage system and helps to increase the air flow through the soil particles.

Place the tree into the pot and then work fresh soil into and around the root system with the aid of a chopstick. Allow for a small space between the soil level and the top of the pot to allow for watering and stop the compost from being washed away over the side of the pot.

Cover the top of the soil area with 4mm washed gravel which will help to keep the compost moist and control weeds by acting as a mulch.

BASIC SHAPES

The shape you give a bonsai is a matter of personal choice and taste. Initially, however, it is advisable to copy your style on that of an advanced student. But before you attempt to create your own individual shape, you must be aware of the basic set of principles which applies to each bonsai shape.

Start by preparing a framework. Working to angles and to desired boundaries is the simplest way to organize your shape. Decide on the boundaries within which you want to keep, 45 or 90deg, for instance. Then, set boundaries of height, width and depth. You will need to draw a plan which will enable you to put foresight into the basic shape of your bonsai.

I must emphasize the word 'basic' here, meaning the bare skeleton – the main trunk together with its framework of branches. More advanced techniques are covered in Chapter 7.

Drawing Your Plan

Step One

Start by drawing a circle as shown in Fig 11(a). This represents your boundary, showing the height and width of your tree.

Divide the circle horizontally in half (or 180deg) as shown in Fig 11 (b). This will allow you to show the top and bottom sections in more detail and also give you an indication of where the bottom branches should start from. Divide the top right hand of the circle and mark the divisions A, B, C, D and E as shown in Fig 11 (c); A should be at 90deg. Now, with a dotted line, draw the same angles on the left-hand side to produce a mirror image. This gives you the choice of using the right- or left-hand side of the tree (*see* Fig 11 (d)).

Provided that you always work from a base line, more lined angles for the side (lateral) branches can be added at a later stage once you have become accustomed to using a plan. Once you have passed the mainframe stage (trunk and branches) you may continue to build or add on to this framework without the aid of a plan.

Finish off the plan by writing a list below the circle, placing each style next to a letter, such as:

(a)   Formal upright (*Chokkan*)
(b)   Curved trunk or Informal upright (*Moyogi*)
(c)   Slanting (*Shakan*)
(d)   Windswept (*Fukinagashi*)
(e)   Cascade (*Han-Kengai*)

Step Two

The second step of our plan is to form a boundary to indicate the height, width and depth of the bonsai shape and to do this we will need to draw a second circle, similar to the first. The first circle is marked with your angles and letters and will be called the 'first

[19]

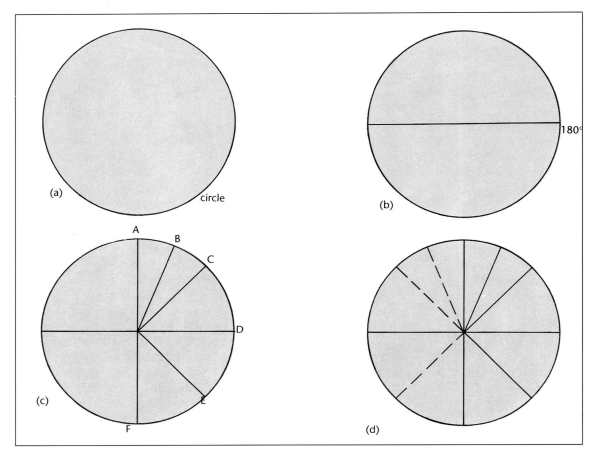

Figs 11(a), (b), (c) and (d)   The beginnings of a drawing plan.

dimension' circle from now on. It will be used to show the boundary from the bottom to the top plus the sides (height and width) and angles of the trunk and branches of the tree. The second circle, or 'second dimension' circle as it will be termed from now on, will be used horizontally to show the boundary from the front to the back and sides (depth and width) and also includes the position for the base of the tree. The rim of the circle is termed the 'boundary line'. It is the main factor in the second dimension circle because it is the point at which the branches will be stopped (*see* Fig 12(a)). The angles are used to show the spacing of the branches from a bird's-eye view, as shown in Fig 12 (b).

Now, by using the two principles of angle and boundary, practise drawing a plan of the style and outline shape of your bonsai as shown in the example Fig 12 (a) and (b).

THE BEGINNING OF A STYLE

Your starting material can be a seedling produced from seed, from striking cuttings, or purchased from a nursery as a one- to three-year-old seedling. It will not make any dif-

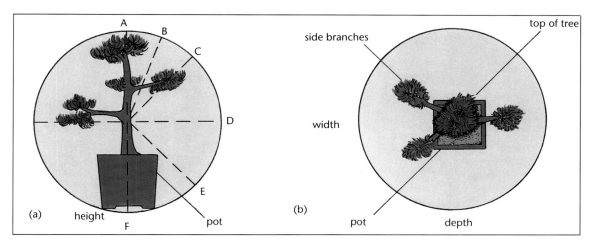

Fig 12 Plan showing height, width and boundary of a formal upright tree.(a) First dimensional plan showing the branch angles. (b) Second dimensional plan, showing the boundary line.

ference, provided that the style you are looking for (for example a straight trunk is needed for a formal upright) is originally present in the seedling. You should also be looking for good strong side growth, or buds which will produce side growth. These should be in odd numbers three, five, seven, etc, to avoid forming a cartwheel effect. However, there is no reason why you cannot pick a seedling with an even number of branches and remove the desired number at the right time of the year.

Formal Upright (Chokkan)

Preparation

When you have selected the suitable seedling with a straight trunk (if possible) and you have familiarized yourself with the pruning techniques and bud rubbing, start by drawing a plan showing the height and width of your tree. On completion of your circle showing these boundaries, pencil in the main trunk at an upright, 90deg angle. You may, if you wish, draw in the pot, container or the root ball, and by doing so you

will indicate the distance from the soil level to the first or lowest branch. You must indicate on your plan the point at which the lowest branch will start, because all buds or growth below this point will be removed to expose a clean trunk.

Continue to draw in the side branches, using odd numbers at 180deg. This is your

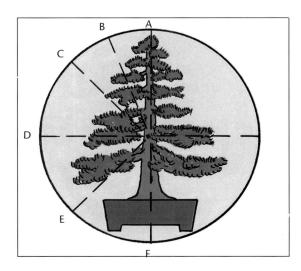

Fig 13 Formal upright style (Chokkan).

[21]

first dimensional plan indicating the height, width and angle of the trunk and side branches. Building a network on top of the upward-facing side of these branches will follow at a later stage.

Next, draw a second dimensional plan or 'bird's-eye view', showing the width (front and back as well as sides) and position of the tree in its pot, as shown in Fig 14. Again, you can apply angles to this plan to show the front, side and back growth. Some trees may be created without the use of either front or back angles, which allows the tree to be turned around each way, ensuring all-round light to the tree.

Draw another circle, but this time looking preferably down from the top of the tree, a view and an angle most people will not see, but which are important from a growing point of view.

With the exception of the windswept style (*Fukinagashi*), the second dimensional plan will only be used to show the position of the trunk's base (the bottom of the trunk) when repotted. When the tree is placed into a bonsai pot, positioning of the trunk (in

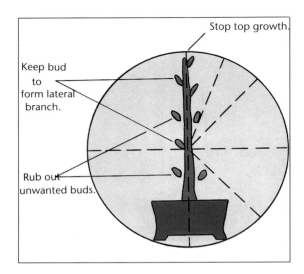

Fig 15   After choosing the buds you wish to keep, rub out the unwanted ones.

most cases slightly off centre) is an important factor; it is of less importance when using a training pot.

Next, mark on your plan the chosen buds or young growth which will produce the side growth on the main trunk, indicating the points at which the main-frame branches will start (*see* Fig 15). Keep the chosen buds and remove the rest, leaving a clean trunk except at the point shown on your plan.

Care

Allow these side branches to develop during the first year to the width defined by the boundary line of your first dimensional plan. Once they have reached the boundary line, each branch is stopped by pinching out the growing tip. This will in turn cause the buds lower down the branch to activate and push out sublateral growth. This method can be repeated, encouraging new growth all the time.

Using the second dimensional plan, allow the sublateral branches to reach their desired points either to the boundary line or to

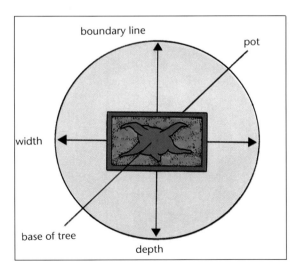

Fig 14   The second dimensional plan, or bird's-eye view, looking down from the top of the tree.

a point inside the boundary line. These in turn are then stopped to encourage further growth, thereby producing lateral, sub-lateral branches and so on, until a complete network of fine branches is formed.

Continue to prune and style your bonsai until you have reached the basic, desired formal upright shape. This may take between five to seven years to form, although starting with a nursery tree rather than seed or cuttings can shorten the process. When you have formed the basic shape and built a fine network of branches, there only remains to control the new growth to maintain the desired shape.

Aftercare
If, during any of the shaping and styling stages, the tree should start to look unwell and show signs of poor growth, stop all forms of training until such time as the tree has recovered and started to put on new, strong growth. You should follow a feeding and watering programme throughout the year and regularly check and spray for pest and disease.

Informal Upright (Moyogi)

The informal upright is basically the same as the formal upright as far as the spacing and number of branches are concerned, but the shape of the trunk is curved rather than straight. When it comes to choosing the height, width, depth and buds to produce the side branches, follow the same pattern as for the formal upright.

The trunk of the informal upright is allowed to curve with a slight twist, allowing for a more flowing style than that of the formal upright. To form the shape of the trunk, you may, if you wish, prune to a bud (the trunk is cut or pruned back to a bud which is facing the direction in which you want the trunk to grow). However, this tends to give a formal 'Z' blocked shape, so that wiring or clamping would be a more suitable path to follow for the informal upright style.

Preparation

As before, start by drawing your first and second dimensional plans, marking in the lines as shown at the beginning of this chapter. After you have finished marking all the lines, a, b, c etc., pencil in the trunk and note the difference between the formal and informal trunk. The branches can be displayed on your plan, remembering to space them alternately. The side branches which should be of an odd number should also be trained on an angle similar to the cascade line (d), as shown at the beginning of this chapter, and also with a slight bend.

Using the second dimensional plan, mark in the position of the base of the tree, width and depth, then pencil in the trunk showing it as a spiral. Next, add an odd number of side branches, and sublateral branches as you did with the formal upright.

Fig 16 Curved, informal upright trunk (*Moyogi*).

Care

Find a suitable nursery stock seedling with a flexible trunk (trees over three years old are not suitable for the beginner) or propagate a seedling slightly taller than shown on your plan, remembering to allow for the tree dropping in height because of the spiral effect. The seedling you are looking for is between one and two years old. At this stage the trunk should still be pliable, therefore allowing you to bend and twist to the desired shape without too much force. Older trees may need either a very thick grade of wire or two grades of wire combined together. In some cases a clamp may be needed. Remember, the most important point when wiring is to anchor the wire, so push the wire deep into the bottom of the pot or through the drainage hole and anchor it before placing the tree into its training pot. Once you are happy that the wire is anchored, start positioning the wire up the trunk, remembering not to cover the growing point for the side branches.

Now comes the most delicate phase, bending the trunk at the points you have chosen on your plan and at the same time pushing the trunk of the tree down to shape it into a spiral shape. Once the desired shape has been reached, pinch out the growing points if they still extend above the boundary line of the first dimensional plan. The chosen odd-numbered side branches can be wired using the two-branch system as shown on page 16. Again, stop the growth from going beyond the boundary line which will also encourage new, lateral growth.

Aftercare
Remove the wire at the end of one growing season or sooner if it is damaging the bark in any way. Follow a watering, feeding and spraying programme for pest and disease throughout the year.

Continue to shape by stopping and rubbing out new growth, followed each year by any further wiring training. Once the tree has reached its desired shape, pruning back and maintaining new growth to keep the tree in its style is the only form of training needed.

Round Head or Broom Style (Hokidachi)

When first attempting the broom style (*Hokidachi*), you should start with a tree which lends itself to this style such as a myrthus for the indoor bonsai and a zelkova for the hardy bonsai. The zelkova is an easy tree to find if you visit a tree nursery or bonsai centre and it can also be easily propagated from seed or cuttings. The myrthus can in most cases only be found at a bonsai nursery or by propagating from seed or cuttings.

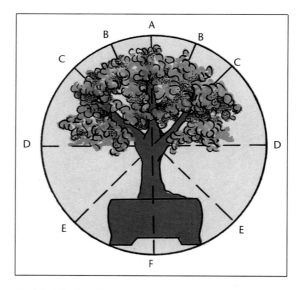

Fig 17   The first dimensional plan of a round head (broom) style (*Hokidachi*).

Broom style myrthus   Start by propagating from seed, cuttings or by purchasing a small myrthus seedling. If you are growing from seed or cuttings, do not prune the roots during the first year, but if you purchase a seedling, try as far as possible to buy it at the beginning of the year (March–April). The seedling should be at least one year old to root-prune straight away. If younger than one year, wait until the following March before touching the root system, but continue to shape and style the top of the tree. (*See* root pruning on pages 17–19).

Broom style zelkova The most important point in creating a broom zelkova is that on a clean, straight trunk a circular network of fan-spaced branches should spring with an abundance of very fine, twiggy branches at their tips. A young zelkova will lend itself to form such a trunk quite easily by cleaning away all growing points to a desired height and then placing a cane along the side of the trunk to train it in a straight manner.

Preparation

Start by using the first and second dimensional plans and show the angles, boundary, height, width and depth of the broom style you are forming. The suggested height would be between 15–30cm (6–12in). Again, by using the plan, choose the trunk's angle. This may be straight (90deg) in the case of the zelkova, or have a slight slant (between 90 and 45deg) for the myrthus.

The next important step is to plan the point from which the branches will start to form the broom-shaped head. This is done by removing all the buds up to a chosen point and encouraging several buds, all at the same level, to produce the network of main branches. This is a totally different practice to the staggered bud and branch system of the formal and informal upright, since you are creating a cartwheel effect.

Once you have chosen three to five buds around the neck of the trunk, mark them in on your first dimensional plan. They will form the main branch system, which in turn will produce sublateral branches. These will,

Fig 18 Soft-pinching myrtle between finger and thumb.

in three to four years, produce a bonsai with a rounded head.

Care

Once you are satisfied with your plan and have found a suitable seedling, follow your plan as closely as possible by taking out unwanted growth by pinching out and removing buds. Prune back to the growing tips and appointed areas as pencilled in on your plans. Again for those who have not read through the section on pinching out the top growth, it is advisable to do so before attempting to go any further.

> **Aftercare**
> If, during any of the shaping and styling stages, the tree should start to look unwell and show signs of poor growth, stop all forms of training until the tree has recovered and started to put on new, strong growth. You should follow a feeding and watering programme throughout the year and regularly check and spray for pest and disease.

[25]

Windswept (Fukinagashi)

In open, exposed, windswept areas such as cliff tops, downs and large open spaces, trees and their branches will grow bent and twisted and will usually be pulled in one direction, away from their exposed side. This is the shape you will be trying to create, and once you are more proficient in the art of bonsai, you will apply *Jins* to create a broken, splintered branch to give the illusion that the tree is growing in wild, barren conditions. A shallow or unusual-shaped dish will help to create that illusion. The tree can be placed at one end of a pot on a slant, with its branches allowed to extend almost to the other end of the dish. If you choose to use a training pot for the first five years, a seed tray with extra drainage holes will serve the purpose as well as the oval pot.

Preparation
Make a first dimensional plan and a second dimensional plan to give you some idea of the overall design. The plans should show

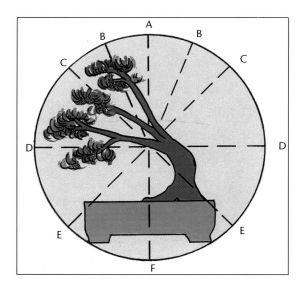

Fig 19   The first dimensional plan of a windswept style (*Fukinagashi*).

height, width, depth, the buds that need to be trained and those that need to be removed. With this particular style, it is very important that you show the position of the tree in its pot right from the start. (If a training pot is used, then the right shape of container should be found.)

Care
If you do decide to purchase your seedling, try as far as possible to choose one whose trunk is slanted. To find such a tree, it might be worth your while looking through the nursery throw-outs. However, make sure that apart from the slanting trunk, the tree shows no other sign of damage. If you enjoy growing from seed or cuttings, wait until the bark becomes woody, then wire the trunk and bend it to the desired shape and angle.

After removing all unwanted growth, allow the planned side branches to reach the points you have chosen inside your boundary line before stopping them to form sub-lateral branches. Some styles require training to buds rather than wiring, but in the case of the windswept style, the branches should look as if they have been bent and twisted by wind turbulence, so that the branches will at some stage need wiring and twisting to create that illusion.

Once you have created your basic shape, which may take as long as five years, continue to remove unwanted new growth only; root-prune if it is the right time of year and repot (*see* pages 17–19). Remember to keep the trunk to the angle shown on your first dimensional plan.

> **Aftercare**
> A feeding, watering and pest and disease programme should be followed throughout the year.

Cascade (Kengai) and Semi-Cascade (Han-Kengai)

The cascade style (*Kengai*) not to be confused with the semi-cascade style (*Han-kengai*), resembles in many ways a one-sided weeping tree. The branches form floral pads of foliage which in most cases extend past the base of the pot. This is one reason for using a tall pot especially made for this style. (Tables are used in some cases which allows the branches to almost reach ground level.)

The semi-cascade, like the cascade, is grown in a tall pot, but its branches tend to fall in a more horizontal fashion than the steep fall of the cascades.

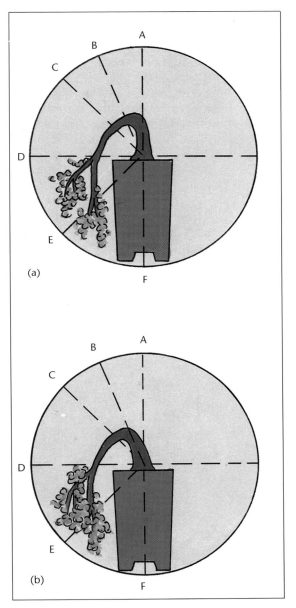

Figs 21 (a) and (b)   Cascade (*Kengai*) and semi-cascade (*Han-kengai*) styles. Note that the *Han-kengai* cascades more to a 45 degree angle.

Fig 20   A cascade-style juniper grown from garden centre stock.

Preparation

This applies to both the cascade and semi-cascade styles. Start by drawing a plan to show all the boundaries and angles, you will need to show the height of the pot on your plan (which in most cases is from the base of the circle up to the horizontal line in the centre of the circle). In the semi-cascade style, the pot takes up the bottom section of the circle.

Root Pruning

This form of root pruning applies to both *Kengai* and *Han-kengai*. The reason for this slightly different style of root pruning is because the cascade style lends itself to a tall pot; in other words, this style will need a longer root system to hold the tree in its pot, rather than the ball-shape you would use when growing other styles, such as a formal or informal upright.

The procedure is basically the same as that for normal root pruning: you still follow the same method of removing the tree from its pot, checking for pests and disease, then loosening the root system. During the first two years or until the root system reaches the bottom of the pot, you will loosen one-third or more of the root system as normal. Where the difference lies is that instead of cutting the complete one-third section of the roots, you will tease the larger or thicker woody roots away from the fine roots and only take out the large woody or thick roots.

Once the root system has formed a complete network of fibrous root hairs throughout the complete length of the tall cascade pot (or once a long vertical root system rather than a horizontal root system has been created), follow the normal root pruning procedure: loosen and remove one-third of the root system, but without losing the length needed to hold the tree in its pot.

Once you have decided on the angles and boundaries, continue to create your style on your plan, allowing for the pot and the length of the branches if growing a full cascade (*Kengai*). With both styles (*Kengai* or *Han-kengai*), the first few centimetres from the base of the trunk may be trained at the angle of a formal upright, informal upright, or slanting. All the buds below the point at which the trunk bends should be taken out. This leaves a clean trunk from its base at soil level to the point from which it bends or starts to cascade downwards.

Once you have specified that point, pencil in the trunk following the angle. When you have finished marking the trunk, define which buds should be left to grow and which should be taken out. The buds that you keep are the starting points for the main and sublateral branches. The latter will flow to form a downward 'step', and will form themselves into pads (*see* Chapter 7).

When you have finished your plan and found starting material (seed, cutting or nursery stock) root-prune if it is the right time of year (March–early April) as advocated, taking out large or thick woody roots. Repot and start shaping, following your plan as closely as possible. Allow the buds or growing points to grow until they reach the desired boundaries and then stop their growing tips to produce sub-lateral branches and pads.

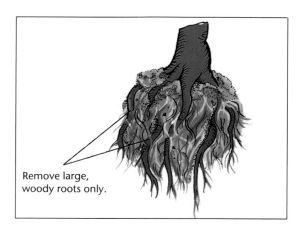

Remove large, woody roots only.

Fig 22　When growing a cascade shape, only the large, thick, woody roots should be removed. The fibrous root system should be encouraged to extend the full length of the pot.

Aftercare
Follow a watering, feeding and pest and disease spraying programme throughout the year.

A List of Bonsai Names and Styles

Bankan   Twisted trunk, often used for shaping pine trees. The twist is more exaggerated than informal upright.

Bonkei   Landscape – a collection of different species of trees in one dish.

Bunjingi   *see* Literati.

Chokkan   Formal upright – the trunk is straight.

Fukinagashi   Windswept – the branches grow to one side of tree, imitating trees found on hill-sides or coast line, which are beaten by strong winds.

Han-Kengai   Semi-cascade – the trunk grows downwards but not as far as a full cascade.

Hokidachi   Broom – the branches form a rounded 'broom' shape.

Ikadabuki   Raft – the trunk leans on its side and the branches are only allowed to develop on one side, giving the illusion of several trees growing in a clump.

Ishitsuki   Tree planted on rock.

Kabudachi   Multiple trunk – a single tree at the base splitting into several trunks to form a group.

Kengai   Cascade – the trunk grows downwards past the depth of the pot.

Korabuki   Group – formed from multiple trunks.

Literati   The tree grows at an angle; the trunk is bare with growth restricted to the top of tree. Sometimes referred to as Bunjingi style.

Moyogi   Curved trunk or informal upright.

Neagari   The main roots are exposed.

Nejikan   The trunk is slightly contorted.

Sabamiki   The bark on the trunk is removed in places.

Saramiki   The bark is completely removed from the trunk.

Sekijoju   Root over rock – the tree is planted over rock and the roots encouraged to grip the rock.

Shakan   Straight trunk, but growing at an angle.

So-kan   Double trunk – trunk starts from one point and splits into two.

Yose-Ue   Group planting.

BONSAI STYLES

I have limited myself to a few of the basic shapes in this chapter because they are easy, basic, 'beginner-friendly' styles to create. In time, you will come to learn other shapes and styles and I have therefore listed many of these above, giving them their Japanese name.

Alternatively, you can try the 'clip-and-grow' style of the Chinese, or consider the new look emerging from the western regions of the world, created around the basic tree and shrub shape.

Chapter 2

SOIL

The most important step to growing a bonsai is to understand a little about the large number of growing mediums used. At the same time, you need to look at the feeds and how they are employed in the made-up soil. This may seem technical, especially to beginners confronted with terms such as loam soils, loamless soils, even soil-less soils, Japanese river sands and Chinese clay, all of which add to the confusion. Bear with me and you will find that soil and feeding are not as puzzling as you might think, once each section of the soil and its function are clarified.

The type of soil you use is very important and only when you have found the right balance will you be able to produce a healthy bonsai. The soils, or to use the correct term 'compost', mentioned in this book are soils that I have used over the past twenty years or so. They are based on sound, tried-and-tested horticultural knowledge and have proved more successful than many so-called 'magic potions'. All the materials used in making compost were chosen from ready-made commercial material, which will avoid the confusing and drawn-out process of sterilizing garden soil and leaf mould. However, if you have the time and room and wish to follow the organic soil route, read through the section on pages 35–41.

The soil used for growing your bonsai is unlike the normal houseplant compost which is basically made up of peat and sand (loamless) and therefore far too light to hold the tree in its pot. The compost we are looking for should contain loam and should be an open compost, allowing air and water to pass through freely, but it should at the same time have adequate moisture-retention properties. Your compost should therefore have a balance of loam to give it body, peat to hold the water and sand to help drainage, assisting the air passage through the compost and generally helping with the physical condition of the particles when placed together.

SOIL TEXTURE

'Soil texture', used in the horticultural sense, relates to the different forms of particles such as sand, grit, clay, humus and also to the size of the particle and the amounts contained in that class of soil. As bonsai growers, we can use the same system to relate to our bonsai compost. In other words, if a compost has a high sand content, it is said to be a sandy compost, or if it has a high percentage of clay, it is called a clay compost. Therefore, if a compost is described as a clay compost, you know that it has poor drainage and air flow, whereas a sandy compost should be open, allowing movement of air and water. A sandy compost will need extra feeding and organic substances such as moss peat for moisture retention.

Soil texture can be easily identified by 'feel'. By this, I mean that if you pick up a handful of moist compost and are able to break it up in your hand into crumbs which feel gritty, you have a sandy compost (high in sand particles); a silky feel to the soil will indicate a silty compost, but if the handful of soil remains in a solid lump which feels wet and sticky, then you have a high content of clay in your compost. Therefore, to produce the bonsai compost we are looking for, the right amounts of clay, silt, sand and humus particles need to be in balance.

Clay

You will find in most cases that clay feels heavy, wet and sticky and is often hard to work with. It is termed a 'cold' soil because it takes a long time to warm up in the spring. This would be true of a bonsai compost containing large amounts of clay. The reason for

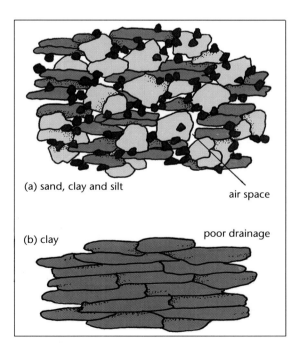

(a) sand, clay and silt

air space

(b) clay

poor drainage

Figs 23 (a) and (b)   Clay particles with very small spaces. An open soil with different-size particles has large spaces in between each particle.

this sticky feel is because clay belongs to a group of sticky paste substances called 'colloids' and because of the sticky, wet and very small particles which are stacked closely together, water and air move very slowly through clay. Clay will also hold moisture to a point that the roots of the tree cannot extract moisture from it.

From this description, it would seem that clay is the major cause of all our compost problems. This may be true in terms of drainage and air flow problems and the compost drying out too quickly, but clay is nevertheless essential for base exchange.

Base Exchange
This is very important. When soluble fertilizers are used, the bases help to stop the fertilizer's particles in the bonsai compost from being washed away (leached) through the drainage system of the compost and drainage hole in the bonsai pot. The particles' core is surrounded by colloids which hold certain material riches or bases such as hydrogen, calcium, potassium, magnesium and sodium. The bases held in the compost are then able to exchange with bases found in the fertilizer, helping them to cling on to the particle.

Silt

Silt is made up of particles as small as 0.002mm. Silt comes from very small grains of silica and larger particles of the very fine silicates. Only when they have blended with clay, sand and humus and gone through further weathering are they useful in a soil. Like the very small particles of clay, silt will hinder the movement of air and water through the compost.

Sand

The sand particles can be divided into two sections, one for fine sand and the other for coarse sand. The ideal soil for our bonsai compost would be a compost with a high percentage of fine sand. Fine sand is able to hold more moisture than coarse sand. Coarse sand, if not supplied with large amounts of organic matter such as moss peat, will dry out very quickly and offer little in the way of plant nutrients. However, coarse sand plays a very important part in the drainage and movement of air through the compost.

Never use builders' sand or gravel (the type used in mixing cement) because of its high lime content. Lime will upset the pH balance and may also form a solid mass. Therefore, always buy your sand and gravel from a garden centre or garden supplies' department and make sure that it reads 'washed horticultural' sand or gravel.

Fig 23 shows two types of soil as seen under a microscope; one is a clay compost and the other contains different size particles. Note how compact the clay particles are as opposed to the large spaces found in an open compost. The spaces in between each particle of the open soil allow air and water to pass freely through the compost, whereas the close spacing found within the clay particles resist water and air movement. A high content of clay in the compost will slow down the movement of air and water. However, as mentioned earlier, it is still beneficial in small amounts because it will help to hold moisture and nutrients around the small sections of gravel and sand. This is another reason for buying a ready-made compost because of a certain amount of clay has been added at the mixing stage.

The following is a list showing the type of tree or shrub and the type of soil it prefers when growing in the wild. Understanding the difference between each tree and soil as well as its pH level will help you when it comes to mixing your bonsai compost. For instance, a beech tree will need a pH level of around 7 and therefore will do well in a compost containing lime and also a fair amount of clay, whereas a rhododendron or azalea needs compost with plenty of sand and a low lime content.

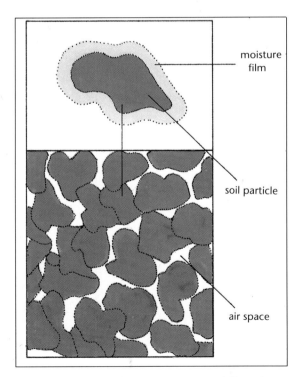

moisture film

soil particle

air space

Fig 24   Soil particles showing air spaces and films of moisture.

pH
The term 'pH' relates to a scale from 1–14 and the number 7 indicates the neutral point. Anything below 7 indicates an acidic compost suited to acid-loving plants, such as rhododendrons. Numbers above 7 imply an alkaline compost. However, the very low and high regions of the scale are totally unsuitable for growing any plant. Most bonsai work on the number range between 6.5 and 7. To find the pH level of your compost, small pH kits can be purchased from your local garden centre.

Clay Soils

TREES

Acer (maple)
Aesculus (horse chestnut)
Alnus (alder)
Carpinus (hornbeam)
Cedrus (cedar)
Chamaecyparis (cypress)
Crataegus (hawthorn)
Cupressocyparis
Cupressus (cypress)
Eucalyptus (gum)
Fagus (beech)
Fraxinus (ash)
Ilex (holly)
Laburnum
Libocedrus
Magnolia (some varieties)
Malus (crab apple)
Picea (fir)
Pinus (pine)
Populus (poplar)
Prunus (cherry)
Quercus (oak)
Salix (willow)
Sorbus (mountain ash)
Taxus (yew)
Thuja
Tilia (lime)
Ulmus (elm)

SHRUBS

Berberis (barberry)
Buddleia (butterfly bush)
Buxus (box)
Ceanothus (California lilac)
Chaenomeles (japonica)
Cornus mas (dogwood)
Corylus (hazel)
Cotinus (smoke tree)
Cotoneaster
Escallonia
Euonymus
Forsythia
Fuchsia
Hamamelis (witch hazel)
Hibiscus syriacus
Ilex (holly)
Jasminum (jasmine)
Juniperus (juniper)
Lavandula (lavender)
Ligustrum (privet)
Lonicera (honeysuckle)
Mahonia
Magnolia (some varieties)
Osmanthus
Philadelphus (mock orange)
Potentilla (cinquefoil)
Pyracantha (firethorn)
Rhus (sumach)
Ribes (currants/ gooseberries)
Rosa (rose)
Rosarinus (rosemary)
Sambucus (elder)
Santolina (cotton lavender)
Spiraea (shrubby meadowsweet)
Symphoricarpos
Syringa (lilac)
Taxus (yew)
Thuja
Viburnum
Weigela

Chalky Soils

TREES

Acer (maple)
Aesculus (horse chestnut)
Carpinus (hornbeam)
Cercis siliquastrum
Cedrus (cedar)
Crataegus oxyacantha
Fagus (beech)
Fraxinus (ash)
Malus (flowering crabs)
Morus nigra
Pinus (pine)
Populus (poplar)
Prunus (cherry)
Salix (willow)
Sorbus (mountain ash)
Taxus (yew)
Thuja
Tilia (lime)
Ulmus (elm)

SHRUBS

Berberis
Buddleia
Buxus (box)
Ceanothus
Cornus mas (dogwood)
Cotoneaster
Euonymus
Forsythia
Fuchsia
Hebe (Veronica)
Hibiscus
Juniperus (juniper)
Lonicera
Mahonia
Olearia
Paeonia
Philadelphus (mock orange)
Potentilla
Prunus (cherry tree)
Pyracantha (firethorn)
Rhus (sumach)
Ribes
Rosa (rose)
Rosmarinus (rosemary)
Sambucus (elder)
Sarcococca (Christmas box)
Spiraea
Symphoricarpos
Syringa (lilac)
Weigela

Sandy Soils

TREES

Acer negundo
Aesculus (horse chestnut)
Ailanthus altissima (tree of heaven)
Arctostaphylos
Betula (birch)
Castanea (chestnut)
Cercis (Judas tree)
Gleditsia
Ilex aquifolim
Magnolia
Nyssa
Platanus (plane)
Populus (poplar)
Populus canescens
Populus tremula
Robinia (false acacia)
Ulmus pumila

SHRUBS

Acer ginnala
Berberis (barberry)
Camellia
Caragana (pea tree)
Cercis (Judas tree)
Cotoneaster
Hibiscus
Ilex crenata
Kerria japonica
Lonicera
Magnolia
Pernettya mucronata
Pernettya prostrata
Rhododendron
Salix caprea
Salix cinerea oleifolia
Salix repens
Viburnum
Wisteria

COMPOST AND AIR FLOW

Air plays a very important part in the health of the tree, more so with the indoor bonsai than with the hardy outdoor. The movement of air in the compost and around the indoor bonsai is far less than the air flow around the outdoor bonsai, therefore ventilation combined with an open compost is an important factor. I found that trees standing on benches which allowed air to circulate the underside of the pot, looked far healthier than those standing on a solid bench, grass area or concrete.

COMPOST AND MOISTURE

The moisture content of a compost is very important. It helps to keep the cell system solid (turgid) and dissolves the nutrients so that roots can take them in. Forget about the amount of water applied to the soil and think in terms of how much water surrounds each particle that makes up the compost. Only then will you see how the combined system (moisture, particle and roots) works. With an open soil, moisture which is not attracted to the particle is drained through the drainage hole at the bottom of the pot.

In Fig 25, the large particle to the left of the diagram shows the film of water around the particle. This is where the tree starts to take in moisture and dissolved nutrients through its root hairs. This process is called osmosis.

Standing the bonsai in a tray of water is not such a good idea, although this practice has been applied to many houseplants over a great period of years. Many problems can arise by blocking drainage holes at the bottom of the pot, which hinders both drainage and air flow. Stagnant water held in the film around the soil particles can give off toxic fumes and cause the roots to rot. Therefore,

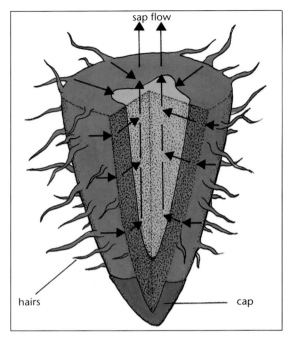

Fig 25   Root hairs are the most important part of the root system in bonsai.

always raise the pot above the water level when using a humidity tray. Always water from the top of the pot and only in extreme cases of dryness (which should never be allowed to happen), will the tree need watering by capillary action by placing the pot into a tub for a short period.

Capillary Action
The rise of water upwards and sideways (as moisture through tissue paper) from the bottom to the top of the pot. This is ideal when watering very fine seeds, but a practice I am reluctant to use when watering bonsai.

The bonsai compost we are looking for should be free from weeds, pests and diseases. Soil taken from the garden should not be used unless partially sterilized first to avoid these problems. Garden soil may also contain toxic waste such as weedkiller which has seeped out from the lawn through capillary action.

A 'sterile' compost literally means a barren, lifeless soil, completely unsuitable for a tree's existence. Partially sterilizing a soil by heat or chemical action will free it of harmful organisms. However, using a compost containing loam will save you the time and expense of partially sterilizing your garden soil.

If you do wish to sterilize your own soil, then a sterilizing unit would be ideal (*see* page 44). The materials used in making one of the ready-made loam composts purchased from a garden centre are loam, peat and sand (sterilized so as to be free from weeds, pests and disease) to which a balance of plant nutrients is then added.

LOAM

Loam is produced by stacking turf upside down in layers, with decomposed straw or animal bedding lying in between each layer. Loam produced by this method takes about six to seven months, which is a long and costly process and one of the reasons why there are so many loamless composts on the market.

Before trying to make your own loam, remember that it takes time and that you will need to add lime to balance the pH to about 6.3, and that it will need sterilizing in addition. Therefore, it is far easier to purchase one of the composts containing loam from your local garden centre as a starting base to your own compost (unless you wish to produce your own organic compost, as set out on page 44). The closest compost containing the different-size particles is a John Innes compost, which has been formalized and used by gardeners all over the world.

John Innes

'John Innes' is not a brand name but a formula used by many different companies and, therefore, good and bad quality bags of John Innes can be found in garden centres.

The John Innes range of compost is divided into four grades – a seed compost and numbers 1, 2 and 3. The higher the number, the larger the amount of fertilizer contained. For example, a No 1 compost contains less fertilizer than a No 3. However, the seed compost has very little in the way of fertilizer, because the seed has a food storage in its seed coat. By using a John Innes seed compost as opposed to 1, 2, or 3, you are starting with a fairly neutral compost to which nutrients can be added at a later stage.

PEAT

There is concern over the dwindling number of peat bogs and the wildlife and fauna associated with them. We should therefore, as far as possible, try to use some form of alternative to peat in our compost, although peat is still most commonly used. Alternatives to peat include beech leaves, hawthorn leaves and coconut fibres (coir).

There are two types of peat: moss peat, which is light brown in colour and looks like flakes of tobacco; and sedge peat, which appears black and sooty in texture and can turn to dust when dry. Always use moss peat; it will cost more but has the heaviness and 'body' required for our bonsai compost.

ORGANIC COMPOST

Leaf mould This is made up of leaves broken down through composting (stacked in layers and allowed to rot down to form a black tar-like humus) and sometimes added to a bonsai compost to give it more body. The type of leaves used will vary the quality of the end result. Leaves from hawthorn and

[35]

beech are excellent. If you do add leaf mould to your compost, make sure it has been partially sterilized before using it. Never use leaves that show signs of disease.

NON-ORGANIC COMPOST MIXTURES

There are five types of compost; seed, cuttings, seedling, light sandy and heavy. Fresh compost containing loam should be purchased from your local garden centre. To prepare, mix in the ratios shown under each section as follows:

Code 1: seed compost If the John Innes seed compost is of good quality it can be used on its own, however, in most cases you will find the need to boost the compost with extra ingredients.
- 100% seed compost if good quality, or
- 80% seed compost,
- 10% moss peat or coconut fibres,
- 10% sharp sand.

Note There are also different forms of volcanic substances available from local garden centres which are suitable for seed sowing.

Code 2: cutting compost
- 50% moss peat or coconut fibres and
- 50% sharp sand.

Note As with seed composts, there are forms of volcanic substances suitable for taking cuttings.

Code 3: open, sandy compost This is a very open compost. A watering programme must be maintained throughout the summer and must winter for indoor bonsai, but less so in the winter for hardy outdoor bonsai. Failure to follow a watering programme will cause the compost to dry out very quickly.
- 60% seed compost containing loam,
- 20% moss peat or coconut fibres and
- 20% sharp sand.

Code 4: medium compost As with a Code 3, a watering programme should be followed.
- 70% seed compost containing loam,
- 15% moss peat or coconut fibres and
- 15% sharp sand.

Code 5: heavy compost This compost, if made correctly, should hold more water than a Code 3 compost, however a watering programme should still be used.
- 80% seed compost containing loam,
- 10% moss peat or coconut fibres and
- 10% sharp sand.

COMPOST MIXING

First find a clean area to mix your compost. This can be a large wooden board or a clean area of concrete. Measure your materials of moss peat, sand, compost containing loam (or leaf mould and other organic substances if used) and place them in a pile next to each other on your clean surface. Start sieving the compost, using a 1.5mm sieve to remove very fine dust particles, followed by the moss peat which should be graded with a 5mm sieve. Mix these two materials together and sieve the combined mixture once

> **Compost mixing**
> Another method for mixing is to use a plastic bag into which all the different materials are placed. The bag is then shaken in order to mix the materials. However, it is better to add moisture to the compost when mixing rather than pot the plant into a dry compost and then water it. This is where problems crop up if using a plastic bag. If you wet the compost in the bag, the soil tends to form sticky small clumps that stick to the sides of the bag and stay in the corners. Therefore, to produce a more even distribution of the moisture and to make life easier, a mixing board is better than a plastic bag.

more through a 1.5mm sieve. Then, add sand to the compost and peat. When all three materials are mixed together in a heap, turn the heap over three times, allowing the materials to form a compost with a combination of large and small particles and an even moisture content. At the end of the mixing you should have a compost that feels gritty, but at the same time silky when flowing through your fingers.

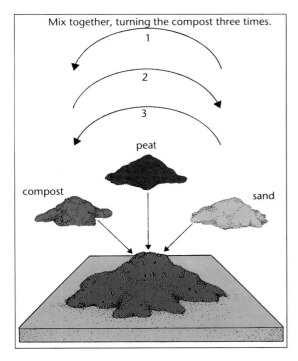

Fig 26 Mixing compost. This should always be done on a clean surface.

FEEDING

Feeding is a very important factor when growing a bonsai, and more so with the indoor bonsai. Although we are trying to slow down the rate of growth on our tree, in real terms we are only talking of height and we are still aiming to produce a thick trunk,

with branches which are proportionately balanced to the thickness of that trunk and a strong, healthy, fibrous root system. Essential nutrients which help to produce such a healthy, well balanced growth and resist diseases are fed into the tree throughout its growing season. These essential nutrients are divided into two types: major elements and trace elements.

Major Elements

The first three major elements are what I term 'invisible' elements (by this I mean they are not mentioned on the feeding packets found at garden centres). They are: carbon, hydrogen and oxygen. Carbon is found in the air which passes through the compost and around the tree. Hydrogen can be found in the water which is applied daily to the compost during the growing season and oxygen is found both in water and air. Therefore, by providing the bonsai with a compost which allows air to pass freely around the soil particles together with the water, you are adding the first of the three major elements.

N.P.K.

The three letters N.P.K. are the chemical symbols for nitrogen, phosphorus and potassium, which are the next three major elements and are applied by feeding.

Nitrogen The bonsai tree will use nitrogen for most of its major growth processes such as the stem and leaves, and it helps to give the tree its green colour by assisting in the formation of chlorophyll (the green colouring-matter found in plants). Care should be taken not to overfeed your bonsai with nitrogen for fear of producing weak, sappy growth, which could be damaged by cold weather, strong winds and pests.

Phosphorus This plays an important role

[37]

in the formation of cells in the young bonsai, particularly in root formation. It may seem strange to encourage the roots to grow when most of the time you are trying to control them, but it is very important that the tree maintains a good, strong, healthy root system to help it through its strenuous training programme during the coming seasons.

Potassium This will help your bonsai through the cold winter spells by controlling sap movement and by building up the tree's resistance to disease.

N.P.K. is widely known by most bonsai growers as the major elements above-mentioned, however there are three other elements which also play their part in the health of your bonsai tree. They are as follows:

Calcium This also helps in the formation of cells and strengthens the tree's structure, developing the growing tips of the tree and its roots.

Magnesium As with nitrogen, magnesium helps to form chlorophyll and works with phosphorus, which in turn assists in seed formation. One of the main causes of yellowing leaves is magnesium deficiency, known as 'chlorosis'.

Sulphur This is used in protein formation and helps the production of oils in the tree.

TRACE ELEMENTS

The bonsai tree will only require small amounts of trace elements such as iron, copper, boron, zinc, manganese and molybdenum. These trace elements work closely with other major elements by speeding up the chemical reaction taking place inside the tree.

Iron and manganese Both help with the formation of chlorophyll and a deficiency will cause yellowing of leaves (chlorosis).

Boron This works with calcium, which strengthens the tree's structure. Boron deficiency will hinder disease protection.

All of the chemical fertilizers used should contain major and trace elements. Be sure to read the packet when purchasing from your local garden centre.
A feeding programme has to take into account the different growth needs of the plant according to different seasons.

Spring High nitrogen content for foliar growth.

Summer Phosphates and potash for the root system. Phosphates and potash strengthen the wood and help the flowering of the plant.

Autumn Potash for the cell system. Potash strengthens the cell system, ready for winter; it also helps to mature woody growth.

By using and combining them with the compost which is low in nutrients as shown earlier in this chapter, it will give you more control over the growth rate during the growing season.
There are two forms of feeding:

1. Foliar feed, where a balance of nutrients enters the plant through the foliage.
2. Root feed; using powder or granule spread over the compost and watered in.

Overfeeding

A plant takes in its water and nutrients (salts) into its cell system through a selectively permeable membrane. This process is known as 'osmosis' (*see* page 34). When the cell can no longer take in water (or in other words when it is full, creating an outward pressure on the wall of the cell), we say that the cell is 'turgid'.

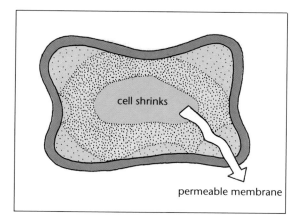

Fig 28   When the cell shrinks, it is termed a 'flaccid' cell.

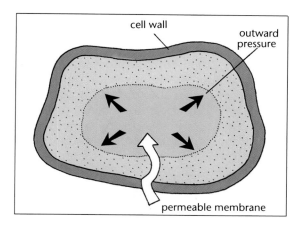

Fig 27   A healthy cell is a turgid cell.

Plasmolysis

If the solution outside the cell becomes more concentrated than the cell sap because of overfeeding, the cell allows water to pass out by osmosis or ex-osmosis which in turn pulls the cytoplasm away from the cell wall, causing the cell to shrink or become 'flaccid', which is one of the main causes of wilting.

Therefore, always follow a feeding programme. (It may be more helpful if the beginner keeps the dilution rate slightly under the recommended level.)

Note   Always read the instructions given on the box, bottle, or packet. Never overfeed your tree, if the growth is too slow and you are working to a feeding programme, do not be tempted to add more feed which can result in root damage and soil contamination. Always use a clean watering-can or sprayer, never use the same container for which you

would use weedkiller, insecticide, or cleaning fluid. Finally, always wash out your container after feeding, then wash your hands with clean water.

Organic Feeds

'Organic feeds' or to give it its full title, 'concentrated organic manures', is a produce from animal and plant residues and should not be classed as organic feeds until these residues have decomposed after being mixed with a compost.

You may also come across organic manures such as hoof and horn, dried blood and bone-meal which can be added to the compost. These organic feeds are not as easy to use as you might think and totally different to feeding a large open area of soil in the garden. Untold damage may result through the compost becoming toxic, so here is a basic set of rules to follow:

1.   Always ask to see a tree that has been planted in such a soil then, if the tree looks healthy, ask for the grower's advice, and then practise on old material before using your best or favourite tree.
2.   Always make sure that the organic sub-

Important!
Always read the instructions given on the box, bottle or packet. Never overfeed your tree. If the growth is too slow and you are working to a feeding programme, do not be tempted to add more feed. This can result in root damage and soil contamination.

Always use a clean watering-can or sprayer. Never use the same container for which you would use weedkiller, insecticide or cleaning fluid. Finally, always wash out your container after feeding, then wash your hands with clean water.

stances are from the current year's stock and that they are in a dry condition before use.
3. Read through the following list of organic substances before attempting to use them. Try to work out the amounts of nitrogen, phosphates and potash you are adding to the soil and remember the amounts of N.P.K. already present in the compost, unless you are using a compost totally free of plant nutrients.

Organic Substances

Hoof and horn (N plus small amounts of P) Mainly nitrogen (between 5–7 per cent) with far smaller amounts of phosphorus acid. When added to a standard potting compost without being completely free of nutrients, the rate applied is 1.25kg per cubic metre.

Dried blood (N plus small amounts of P) Dried blood is a quick-acting organic feed containing 7–14 per cent nitrogen with 1–2 per cent phosphoric acid. Mainly applied as a top dressing (placed on top of the compost surface) at 17–34g per square metre. If the calculations prove too much for you, follow this simple guide: mark a piece of card dividing the surface area of the square metre into equal sections, then divide by weight the dried blood into equal amounts for each section. Now, place your

bonsai tree on to the marked card and apply the top dressing.

Note At first, apply the dressing slightly under the rate shown above.

Fish guano The older Japanese practices of feeding would have used this form of organic food, which they term as fish meal. After the oil has been extracted from the fish, it is dried and ground down to a powder. This powder should contain approximately equal amounts of nitrogen (6–9 per cent) and phosphoric acid (6–9 per cent). This produces a balanced feed containing the important N and P, which is fast-acting as well as long-lasting. The only problem is the lack of potash (K), but if you read on, wood ash will provide the third important ingredient.

Wood ash Wood ash is produced by burning clean, healthy branches. This ash is rich in mineral salts, the most important being potash (1–7 per cent). Wood ash is then applied at the rate of 135 to 270g per square metre. The soluble state of wood ash means that the salts are very quick-acting. If you do attempt to manufacture your own wood ash, take the following into account:

1. For those young bonsai growers, I would strongly recommend that an adult supervises the burning of the wood.
2. Never add petrol, paraffin or rubber tyres to the fire. The fire should be totally free from objects such as wire and plastic. Clean paper should be the only form of lighting material.
3. Make sure the fire is contained within a specific area, away from objects which may explode or catch fire. If possible, build a fire area similar to that for a barbecue. Use fire bricks.
4. Allow the fire area to cool down before attempting to collect the ash.

[40]

5. Store the ash in a clean, dry area, away from children and pets.

Unsuitable Organic Feeds

Bone-meal (P plus small amounts of N) Bone-meal is not the most practical organic feed to use for growing bonsai. The reason for this is because it is a very slow-acting form of phosphoric acid feed containing 20–25 per cent phosphoric acid and smaller amounts of nitrogen (approximately 3–4 per cent). The problem for the bonsai grower lies in mixing the bone meal far enough in advance to allow for it to break down, ready for the tree to take in the phosphoric acid. If added to a compost at a very early stage and allowed to stand for several months, bone-meal would prove totally unsuitable, since the compost would become too toxic through the reaction of the different feeds mixing together and not being used. It would therefore be far better to find alternative forms of phosphoric acid

through a normal packet feed containing N.P.K. plus trace elements.

Poultry manure (N plus P) This form of feed, if given when fresh, will seriously damage the fine fibrous root system of the bonsai. Although high in nitrogen and phosphoric acid, poultry manure is best avoided, unless a careful study has been carried out into the effect this feed will have on the tree's growth.

Farmyard Manure (FYM) FYM is used as a *soil* conditioner and is therefore neither suitable for bonsai as a *compost* conditioner nor as a form of food, basically because of its low content of N.P.K. A small sample test will reveal contents of:

*   N: 0.4–0.6%
*   P: 0.2–0.3%
*   K: 0.5–0.7%

FYM is therefore best left out of your bonsai practice.

Chapter 3

PROPAGATION

Starting material for a bonsai can be obtained from a variety of sources: either by sowing seeds, striking cuttings, or by techniques such as air-layering, layering or grafting. However, if you neither have green fingers nor the spare time, then starting a bonsai from nursery stock is the answer. In some cases, however, growing from seed may be the only way to obtain the tree you are looking for.

Fig 29   A Japanese maple with spring colours.

SEED COLLECTION

'Bonsai' refers to the process of cultivating a potted plant or tree, and there is therefore no such thing as a genetic bonsai. A seed taken from a bonsai tree or any other tree will not grow into a bonsai without *specialized training*.

There are three ways of obtaining your bonsai seed. You can:

1.   Collect seed from the wild
2.   By seed from your local garden centre or bonsai nursery.
3.   Order seed by post from a seed supplier.

Wild Seeds

Different rules apply to different parts of the world; in some cases there may be no need for permission to collect seed, but in Britain, for example, permission is needed in most cases to collect from woods, parks or private gardens.

Seed collection time depends on the type of tree or shrub and its flowering period. In most cases, you will find that a lot of the tree and shrub seeds are ready from late summer to autumn, before they go into dormancy.

Dormancy is a period in which the seeds are naturally protected against external conditions until ripe for germination and able to take on different conditions such as cold, heat, and moisture. Seeds should therefore be gathered before they start to ripen. If the seeds have started their dormancy period, you will need to stratify them.

STRATIFICATION

This is a process used to overcome dormancy and to do this you will need either a seed tray or a pot, some peat and some horticultural sharp sand.

Use one part peat to three parts sand, then mix the two together and fill a seed tray that has a depth of 7.5cm (3in) and drainage holes at the bottom.

First, spread a 2.5cm (1in) layer of the peat/sand mixture over the bottom of the seed tray, then place a layer of seeds and cover with a second 2.5cm (1in) layer of the mixture, followed by a second layer of seed and so on until you have filled the seed tray.

There are two ways in which to imitate a cold period:

1. By placing the seed tray into a refrigerator with a temperature ranging between 1–4°C (30–40°F) for a period of four to six weeks.
2. By placing the seed tray outside, in the coldest part of the garden (north-facing if possible). This method is slower than if using a refrigerator, but the end result is better.

I personally prefer the outside placement, because the rise and fall in temperature tends to have angreater effect on the seed-coat, producing a quicker and better germination rate. Seeds such as berberis, cotoneaster, Chinese juniper, crab apple, cherry and pyracantha all need a five to six months' period outside, while some of the seeds, such as horse chestnut and oak, will not store or overwinter. These are collected green and sown outside either in the soil or in pots from September to October.

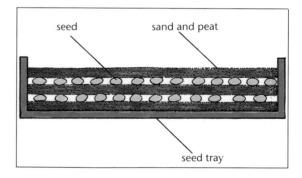

Fig 30 Stratification. To stratify the seeds, place them in the fridge or in the coldest part of the garden during the winter.

Packet Seeds

Not many garden centres stock tree seeds, so that it will be a case of ordering by mail from a seed specialist or bonsai nursery. When you receive the seeds, check the date on the packet to make sure the seeds are fresh. Instructions are supplied with each packet.

There are two main classes of seed: hard, medium and soft. Most seed packets will only give you the common name of the tree, so that I have only used common names in the text below.

Hard seed Oak, elm, horse chestnut, crab apple, beech and maple.

Medium seed Southern beech, bamboo, ginkgo, mulberry, wisteria, tree of heaven, pagoda tree, wattle and Christ's thorn.

Soft seed Acacia, bo tree, kaffir, monkey puzzle, octopus tree, pomegranate and yellow shower tree.

ORGANIC SEED COMPOST FOR BONSAI

If you wish to grow bonsai by organic methods, you will need to produce an organic compost for seed sowing and transplanting. This is quite simply done by using a mixture of horticultural sand and either sterilized garden soil or worm cast.

A good method of sterilizing is to purchase a ready-made sterilizing unit which looks like a bucket and stands on a container full of water. Bottom heat is applied to boil the water. This, in turn, gives off steam, which escapes through small holes in the bottom of the bucket and up through the soil, sterilizing it at the same time. This practice should be carried out in an open area.

Another method is to use one of the volcanic substances purchased from your local garden centre. These can be used as a substitute, but you must remember that there are no nutrients in this compost. The absence of nutrients in the seed compost is not a problem in the early stage because the seed's coat contains some forms of food. However, this is soon used up and the plant will start to show some deficiencies.

Caution!
Never attempt to move (transplant) the seedling until its first set of true leaves (cotyledons) have appeared.

Compost for transplanting

A compost for transplanting the germinated seeds into individual pots can be made up of horticultural sand and sterilized soil or mole hill. Nutrients in the form of concentrated manures (i.e., dried blood, etc.) will need to be applied, at a rate dependent on the size and depth of pot and the type of plant being transplanted.

Basic soil mixture for germination and transplanting (Nutrients will need to be applied to transplanting compost.)
- 80% sterilized garden soil or worm cast and
- 20% horticultural sand.

Hygiene
Never use a seed compost more than once, unless it has been sterilized by steam first. Always use a clean seed tray.

SEED SOWING

There are two types of seed, one which will need the heat and protection of a glasshouse and the other which is a hardier seed and can be sown outside. (Refer to the table on page 47.)

Indoor Seed

Sow these in a seed tray and place in a glasshouse, propagator or coldframe. Bottom heat should be applied. The temperature for general seed sowing should range between 12–18°C (54–64°F), but some of the exotic trees such as baobab, may need a slightly higher temperature (*see* Chapter 9).

Method
Always use a clean seed tray, with plenty of

drainage holes at the bottom. Fill the seed tray to just over half-way with a seed compost (compost Code 1 or organic compost) and firm it down using a firming board. Large seeds should be spaced out over the surface of the compost, as shown, whilst small seeds can be sprinkled, spaced out as much as possible at the same time.

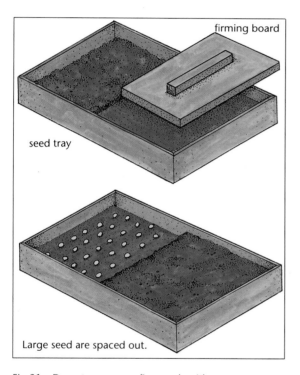

Fig 31   Do not cover very fine seeds with compost.

Cover large seeds with a 5-7cm (¼–½in) layer of compost; small seeds with a fine layer (just enough to cover the seed); while very fine seeds should not be covered. In the case of seeds that are neither large nor fine, the compost should be applied by passing it through a sieve.

Water the seeds, using a watering-can with a fine rose. First, start the water-flow away from the tray, then move it backwards and forwards across the compost area, moving the can away from the tray before it runs out of the water. In this way the water will not form puddles or holes in the compost, which would bury or wash away the seeds.

Outdoor Seed

Hardy outdoor bonsai seeds should be sown in September to October, or March to April. The procedure for outside sowing is the same as for indoor, except that you should apply a little more sharp sand to help the drainage. Use a compost Code 1 or an organic compost; in some cases, the seeds can be sown straight into the soil. Stand the seed tray in a stable and secure place, away from overhanging trees or gutters that may drip, and place them on table or bench, out of the reach of domestic pets. If birds become a problem, nets can be erected.

Damping Off

The most common problem when growing bonsai from seed is the occurrence of a soil-borne fungal disease known as 'damping off' (*Pythium* and *Rhizoctonia solani*). If the stem is damaged at soil level or just above, the roots may rot and leave you with a black stump covered in grey mould (*Botrytis cinerea*). Chemical control, such as you may find on the shelves of garden centres, is not always totally effective. Copper fungicide or a Cheshunt compound backed by good hygiene, such as clean seed trays and partially sterilized compost, offer the best possible prevention against the disease. As far as possible, try to follow the following list:

1.   Always wash seed trays with a horticultural disinfectant before using them.
2.   Never use the same seed compost to sow a second batch of seeds.
3.   Make sure that the tray never becomes waterlogged and try to control the level of humidity, keeping it to a minimum.
4.   Spray with a copper fungicide or Cheshunt compound.

When the seeds have developed their cotyledon and are large enough to handle, prick them out and pot them into small pots, using a compost Code 4 or an organic compost. Care should be taken not to damage the stem when pricking out.

> **Aftercare**
> Protect from strong winds, heavy rain and frost. Look out for pests that will eat young foliage.

Soil-Sown Seeds

A wide variety of seeds can be sown directly into a prepared site. Seeds such as oak and horse chestnut should germinate in the spring without too many problems after being sown in the autumn.

Autumn Sowing

Prepare the bed by digging the soil and removing any weeds, especially those of the perennial type. Firm the soil by walking over the soil surface and pushing down with your heels, taking out any hollows, but be careful not to compact the soil down too hard, otherwise you will impede the drainage (pan the soil).

Make drills about the same depth as the seeds. Using the corner of a draw hoe, carefully space the seed, sowing along the length of the drill. Cover the seed with the soil from the drill and firm it with the back of a rake.

Spring Sowing

The bed for spring planting should be forked over in the late autumn, ready for sowing the following spring. Roughly dig the soil, leaving it in large clumps to be broken down by frost over the winter period.

Lightly fork over the bed, breaking down any large lumps left unaffected by the winter weather. Sow the seed in seed drills, in the same way as for autumn sowing.

Before attempting to sow your seeds, check through the following list to find out when and where to sow them.

NURSERY STOCK

The type of nursery you should be looking for is the smaller retail outlet which propagates and grows-on its own stock of trees and shrubs. There, you should be able to find young, one- to three-year-old seedlings.

The same category of nursery is ideal if you are looking for specimen trees – both container- and soil-grown – which can be maintained at the height they have reached or reduced in size (chopped). Some bonsai growers will use trees up to 3 metres in height.

Fig 32 Zelkova. An attractive tree for both summer and winter.

[46]

PROPAGATION

Tree Seed	March/April	September/October	Outside	Under Cover
Acer (maple)	***			***
Aesculus (horse chestnut)		***	***	
Arbutus (strawberry tree)	***			***
Berberis	***			***
Betula (silver birch)	***		***	
Buxus (box)		***		***
Carpinus (hornbeam)	***		***	
Castanea (sweet chestnut)		***		***
Catalpa (Indian bean)	***		***	
Cedrus (cedar)	***			***
Cercis (Judas tree)	***			***
Chaenomeles	***		***	
Cotoneaster	***		***	
Crataegus (hawthorn)	***		***	
Cryptomeria	***		***	
Cupressus	***		***	
Fagus (beech)	***		***	
Fraxinus (ash)	***	***	***	
Ginkgo (maidenhair tree)	***			***
Ilex (holly)	***		***	
Juglans (walnut)	***		***	
Juniperus (juniper)	***		***	
Laburnum (golden chain)	***		***	
Larix (larch)	***		***	
Liquidambar (sweet gum)	***		***	
Liriodendron (tulip tree)	***		***	
Malus (crab apple)	***		***	
Nothofagus (southern beech)	***		***	
Podocarpus	***			***
Prunus (cherry)	***			***
Pseudotsuga (Douglas fir)	***		***	
Pyracantha (fire thorn)	***			***
Quercus (oak)		***	***	
Rhododendron and *Azalea*	***			***
Rhus (sumach)	***			***
Robinia (false acacia)	***			***
Sequoia (redwood)	***		***	
Sequoiadendron (wellingtonia)	***		***	
Sorbus (mountain ash)	***		***	
Stewartia	***			***
Syringa (lilac)	***			***
Taxodium (swamp cypress)	***			***
Taxus (yew)	***		***	
Tilia (lime)		***	***	
Ulmus (elm)		***	***	
Wisteria	***			***
Zelkova (grey bark elm)	***		***	

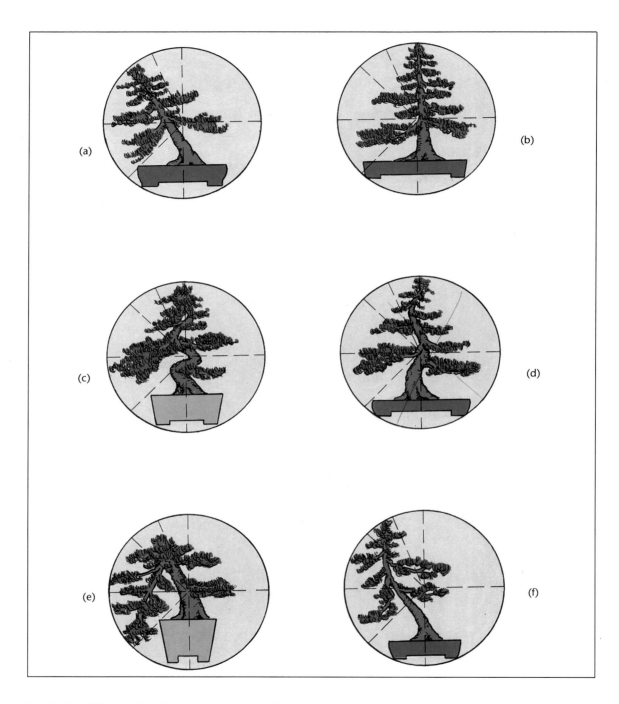

Fig 33   Six different styles of bonsai. (a) Leaning or slanting trunk (*Shakan*). (b) Formal upright
(*Chokkan*). (c) Curving or informal upright trunk (*Moyogi*). (d) Twisted, coiled trunk (*Bankan*).
(e) Cascade style (*Kengai*). (f) Long bare trunk with top growth (*Bunjingi* or *Literati*).

Container Stock

When choosing your nursery stock, try as far as possible to pick a tree that is as close as possible to the shape or style you are looking for. For instance, choose a tree with a curved trunk if you are looking to create an informal upright (*Moyogi*), bending to one side for a windswept style (*Fukinagashi*) or with branches growing downward for a weeping or cascade shape (*Kengai*).

Maintaining Your Nursery Stock

Container stock comes in different forms of containers – the two most commonly used being the plastic liner or the plastic pot. A tree in a plastic liner should be placed into a training pot as soon as possible, but not always root-pruned. Root pruning is best carried out in the spring (March–April). Never attempt to root-prune a deciduous tree in full foliage. If it is the wrong time of year for root pruning, place the tree into a terracotta pot of the same size as the plastic liner. A tree in a plastic pot, on the other hand, can be left in its container until such time as it is ready to be moved into a training pot.

Watering
Winter (October–March) Once or twice a week. Never allow the soil to dry out.

Spring and summer (April–September) Every day, depending on weather conditions. Never allow the soil to dry out.

Feeding
The time for feeding and the type of feed you use depend on the time of year and variety of tree.

Deciduous trees Feeding stops from the end of September throughout the winter until the end of March. From spring until the end of September, follow a feeding programme: high nitrogen content at the beginning of the year to a low nitrogen content from the middle to the end of the year.

Evergreen trees Except for the pine tree which falls under a class of its own (*see*

> **Shape and Style**
> You can start to add the shape and character to your nursery stock tree or shrub from day one, but always make sure that the tree is responding to its new conditions before carrying out any form of pruning.

Chapter 7), most evergreens such as the juniper can be fed in the same way as the deciduous tree.

Chapter 4

CUTTINGS FOR HARDY AND INDOOR BONSAI

In the previous chapter we talked about seed sowing and growing from nursery stock. In this chapter we will look at producing trees from cuttings and will also look at grafting, layering and air-layering.

Growing from cuttings and layering enables you to produce a tree which is identical in colour, foliage, etc., to the tree from which the cutting was taken, whereas only *species* will come true to form from seed.

Grafting is ideal for producing fruiting bonsai or unusual colours, such as the red maple *Acer rubra* grafted on to the green maple *Acer palmatum*; or grafting to produce small pine needles on a thick, rough trunk, such as the white pine *Pinus parviflora*, which produces small needles, grafted on to the black pine, *Pinus thunbergii*, which has been soil-cultivated to create a thick, old-looking trunk.

Air-layering is also a useful practice and one that can be used to reduce a long, 'leggy' trunk or to produce a tree with a thick trunk.

PROPAGATION OF CUTTINGS

Both hardy outdoor and indoor bonsai can be propagated by cuttings, except in the case of hardwood cuttings which only apply to hardy bonsai. Indoor bonsai

Fig 34   White pine grafted on to a black pine rootstock.

material, or less hardy bonsai, can be taken in the same way as the hardy stock, but only as softwood cuttings with bottom heat or as semi-ripe cuttings taken in the summer. The difference comes at the end of the summer when the hardy bonsai will tolerate low temperatures, but the less hardy bonsai material wil require a temperature around 15–21°C (60–70°F) and a frost-free position. As mentioned in Chapter 1, there are three types of cuttings for the hardy bonsai (softwood, semi-ripe and hardwood), but only two are advisable for the indoor bonsai (softwood and semi-ripe).

A softwood cutting is taken from the current season's wood between April and May and also as early as January if kept in the right conditions (if bottom heat is used). Semi-ripe cuttings are also the current season's wood. These cuttings should be taken from July to September and should show a woody base. Hardwood cuttings are the current season's wood in their ripe stage. Most hardwood cuttings will root in the soil without heat or cover from November to December.

Collect strong healthy side-shoots. Place all your collected matter in plastic bags to stop them from drying out and ensure that non-flowering material is always free from pest and disease.

Use a Code 2 cutting compost, mainly containing 50 per cent moss peat and 50 per cent sharp sand (not silver sand). Other volcanic substances can be used instead of the sharp sand and at the rate of:

- 50–75% volcanic material
- 25–50% moss peat

Note You should always use a moss peat and not sedge.

> **Tray or Pot?**
> Either will do. If using a pot, place the cutting around the outside of the pot, which tends to be warmer than the centre; the top section of a plastic bottle will make a cheap form of propagator.

Softwood Cuttings

Preparation
Cut just below a node to a length ranging between 5cm (2in) and 7.5cm (3in). Remove the leaves on the lower part of the cutting. Dip the base of the cutting into a rooting hormone, then push it genty into your cutting compost. Place cutting under mist or on to a warm bench.

Care
If the tips of the cutting are starting to shoot and a white root system can be seen, the cutting has taken. If grown in a tray, remove the cuttings from the tray and pot them individually into small pots containing one of the soils described in Chapter 2.

Semi-Ripe Cuttings

Preparation
The preparation for semi-ripe cuttings is very similar to that for softwood; i.e., node cuttings, but the length is slightly longer, 5–10cm (4–6in). This type of cutting is ideal if you are unable to provide artificial heat.

Care
Check for new growth and a white root-system. If the cuttings have rooted, pot as you would softwood cuttings. If grown in a cold frame, give them ventilation on warm days and start to harden them off ready for the winter. Leave the cuttings to overwinter in the frame until the following spring.

Hardwood Cuttings

Preparation
Hardy bonsai only. Collect hardwood cuttings during November and choose well-ripened cuttings of the current season's wood. The cuttings' length should be between 15–25cm (6–9in).

Care

Leave undisturbed in the soil for one year. After this time, transplant into individual pots.

Training Cuttings

Softwood and Semi-Ripe

Once the cuttings have taken root, move them into individual pots and place them back into the same temperature for the next week or two. Then, move them closer to the door if grown in a glasshouse, leave the top slightly open if grown in a cold frame, or pull back the plastic if grown in a low tunnel. If you have a small propagator, lower the temperature and allow more air to enter. This will give the seedlings a chance to acclimatize themselves to conditions outside the growing area. Pinch out the growing tips during the first year, but do not attempt to root-prune the root-system at this stage. Check the watering on a daily basis and feed with a balanced fertilizer every three weeks. Spray for pests and diseases.

Hardwood

Hardwood cuttings will bypass the hardening-off period, but should still be protected from frost and strong winds. They should be left in the soil after planting in November (year one) to the following March (year three). During this time, the growing tips should be pinched back severely to keep the growth under control. Never allow the compost to dry out and feed every three weeks on a balanced fertilizer. Spray for pests and diseases.

CUTTINGS ON A SMALL SCALE

If you wish to experiment or have neither the room nor time for large-scale propagation, a small propagator or a pot and the top section of a plastic bottle are all that you need.

Training Equipment

Basic Propagator

This is for semi-ripe cuttings only. Either make your own or purchase a plastic pot and cover from your local garden centre.

Fill the pot with a cutting mix Code 2. Choose your semi-ripe cutting material and prepare the cuttings as previously described. When the cuttings are ready, make holes around the outside of the pot with a dibber or chopstick and transplant your cuttings.

Water the compost and allow the excess water to drain away, then secure the plastic top. (Alternatively, secure a plastic bag with a wire frame.) Follow the advice set out in the 'semi-ripe' section.

Electric Propagator

You can purchase this type of propagator from your local garden centre. It will enable you to grow softwood and semi-ripe cutings without too much effort.

Choose your electric propagator carefully and make sure it has a thermostat, so that you have more control over the tempera-

Some Practical Advice
Because your propagator is electrically-powered, it will need to be placed near to a power point, which may be a problem because you will also need to choose an area with plenty of light. You can overcome the problem of the power point by using an extension lead, but remember, *never* allow the extension lead to come into contact with water and *always* extend the cable to its full length, otherwise the cable will overheat and may cause a fire.

If in doubt, do not hesitate to ask the advice of a professional electrician.

ture. You should also look out for ease of access and ventilation facilities.

Using an electric propagator Turn on the propagator and allow the temperature to reach the desired level, depending on the type of cutting and the time of year.

Take your cuttings as described in the softwood or semi-ripe cuttings section, then place the tray or pot into the propagator. With the advantage of bottom heat, cuttings should root in four weeks.

CUTTINGS ON A LARGER SCALE

If you have the space, it is far better to plan and build your own bonsai propagation area, which could also be useful for storage and soil-grown bonsai. The propagation area may typically consist of a glasshouse containing an electric propagator, a warm bench and a mist unit, a cold frame and an open-soil area.

There are five different ways in which I produce my cutting material. The first is with the aid of a mist unit; the second with a warm bench; the third with a cold frame; the fourth with a low polythene tunnel, and the fifth in an open, well-cultivated soil.

The Mist Unit

This is used mainly for softwood cuttings and will prevent moisture-loss in foliage.

The mist unit is a form of bench with electric cables running through a sand and gravel base. The cabels are controlled by a thermostat and the temperature is kept at around 20°C (70°F). A circuit-breaker called an 'electric leaf' is fitted, which turns the mist jets on and off, maintaining the humidity level. You can buy a large misting unit, or a smaller one, which will take 50–100 cuttings.

> **Fog Mist**
> This is almost the same as the mist of the mist unit, but produces a very fine, fog-like mist.

The Warm Bench

This is especially good for material prone to rot in humid conditions, such as the maple. It can also be used for softwood cuttings, provided that they do not thrive on humid conditions.

The warm bench is a bench with sides and a very fine mesh – less than 4mm wide – covering the bottom to allow for drainage. The mesh is itself covered with 6mm gravel, on top of which a thin layer of mixed sand and gravel is then spread. An electric warming cable is then placed on top, coiling in several U shapes, connected at one end to a thermostat which controls the temperature. More sand is added on top of the cables.

When plugged in, the cables heat up the sand and provide bottom heat to the pots containing the cuttings.

The Cold Frame

This is ideal for growing most semi-ripe cuttings. There are many cold frames on the market, so choose carefully. The old brick or wood frame is hard to come by unless you are able to make it yourself. If you buy a cold frame, make sure that it is of good quality, made of brick or wood and lined with polythene. I personally prefer the brick cold frame, because it is easier to maintain than the wood one, which has to be treated regularly. The lid must fit securely, but be easily removed to allow ventilation and hardening off. The bottom of the cold frame will need good drainage. This can be obtained by digging a hole the same shape and size as the cold frame and filling it with hardcore and gravel.

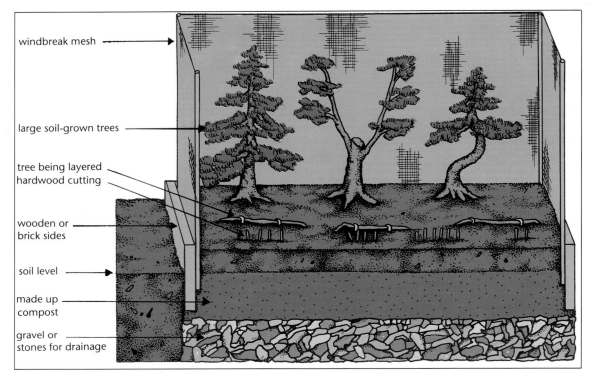

windbreak mesh

large soil-grown trees

tree being layered
hardwood cutting

wooden or
brick sides

soil level

made up
compost

gravel or
stones for drainage

Fig 35 A growing area can be used for growing specimen trees, cuttings, and for layering. By building sides made of wood or brick and adding a good drainage system, you will make the ideal outdoor growing area.

An electric warming cable can be fitted in the bottom of the frame, so that you have both a cold frame *and* a warm bench, which could also be used to overwinter your bonsai during periods of very low temperature.

Low Polythene Tunnels

These are mainly used for semi-ripe cuttings. Temperature control can be a problem during hot summers.

The tunnel can be made of polythene or plastic. In the past, most low tunnels were made of glass, but you will find it less expensive to use either of the other two alternatives. The problem with plastic is that it will not roll back during warm spells in the summer, and I therefore use polythene to cover the tunnel.

Open Ground

Open ground is used for hardwood cuttings.

The area for rooting cuttings in the open should be a sheltered, south-facing aspect, out of heavy shade and strong winds, with good drainage. Removable windbreaks made of mesh should be erected around the sides of the growing area; these will help to reduce moisture-loss from the cutting, as will a top cover, again made from greenhouse mesh shading. The top cover will protect the cutting from the sun's hot rays, thus easing the pressure on the developing root system.

[54]

CUTTINGS LIST

Acer

During April, cuttings of the Japanese maple (*Acer palmatum*) should be placed in a tray with a compost mixture of two-part moss peat to one-part sand. The tray is then placed in any of the following three options:

1. Under mist.
2. On a warm bench, or small propagator.

growing shrub and can make a very interesting bonsai. Hardwood cuttings are taken in November, smaller varities can be propagated by division in April.

Chaenomeles

Known by two other names, Japanese quince and cydonia, *Chaenomeles* will make an attractive flowering bonsai. The flowers are very colourful, but tend to be too large for the tree. Softwood cuttings are

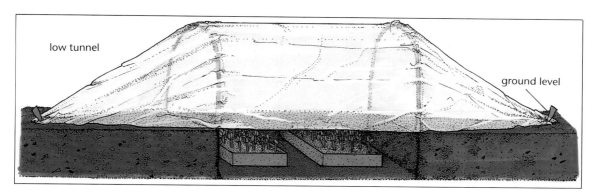

Fig 36   A low polythene tunnel is ideal for semi-ripe cuttings, and does not have to be expensive.

3.   Under a low plastic tunnel in June as a semi-ripe cutting.

I personally prefer to use a warm bench which prevents the maple cuttings from becoming too wet. The cutting should take root after four weeks.

Berberis

These can be taken as hardwood cuttings. Some smaller varieties such as those ending with the name 'Nana', can be propagated by division of the root ball during the autumn.

Buxus

Commonly known as box, it is a very slow-

taken in June and put in a cold frame, a low plastic tunnel or an unheated propagator.

Cornus

The cornus is also called dogwood. The one I use for bonsai training is called *Cornus mas* and produces yellow flowers in February. Hardwood cuttings are taken in November. Cuttings can also be taken in October, but would need to be placed in a cold frame or a small, unheated propagator.

Cotoneaster

Cotoneaster horizontalis is the most popular form in bonsai. With its weeping, herring-bone branch work, it will make a good, in formal bonsai. In addition, it bears white flowers in the spring and red berries in the winter. Cuttings are taken in June and placed under mist, a low plastic tunnel or an unheated propagator.

Jasminum

Jasminum nudiflorum is the best form to use for bonsai. It bears yellow flowers during the early part of the winter, and displays well if grown over rock. Hardwood cuttings are taken in November.

Juniperus

Two forms of juniper are used, *Juniperus chinensis* and *Juniperus rigida*. Cuttings for *J. chinensis* are taken in April and put under mist whilst cuttings for *J. rigida* are placed in a cold frame or small propagator also in April.

LAYERING

Layering is a good alternative to cuttings when trying to propagate bonsai material which tends to be slow or difficult to root. There are several ways of layering such as simple layering, continuous layering (also known as 'French layering') and serpentine layering. The best time to perform layering is between April and July.

Simple Layering

Take a branch and pin it to the surface of the soil, or the soil level if grown in a pot. Once the branch has been pinned, you will need to interrupt the sap flow. This can be accomplished in two ways:

1. By cutting a tongue below the bend.
2. By placing a piece of wire, such as the type used for wiring, around the bark at the bend.

In some layering techniques, such as that used for rhododendrons, a stake is placed at one end.

Continuous Layering

This is almost the same as simple layering, but more pins are used to hold the branch at a horizontal plane. This forces the root-system along the complete length of the underside of the branch, which encourages the buds to grow into upright shoots. When both roots and shoots are showing healthy growth, the rooted section can be cut away from the 'mother' tree and will form the beginnings of a bonsai raft.

Serpentine Layering

This is a good way of producing wisteria and is again very similar to continuous layering. Instead of pinning the branch to the soil, bury chosen sections, leaving a bud showing. This bud will in turn grow into a stem, whilst the buried sections develop a root-system. When the roots and shoots have developed strong, healthy growth, each section is cut away.

AIR-LAYERING

The object of air-layering is to produce a plant by encouraging roots to form from a chosen point, but at the same time allowing the stock plant to provide moisture and nutrients. There are three ways to air-layer. The first is generally used for house plants and good for the beginner to try, the second and third are used by some of the hardy bonsai growers, but are also suitable for indoor bonsai. Many bonsai are started by this process, mainly because it is possible to air-layer old wood as well as young. The young wood will root within twelve months, but older wood may take longer. The advantages of this form of propa-

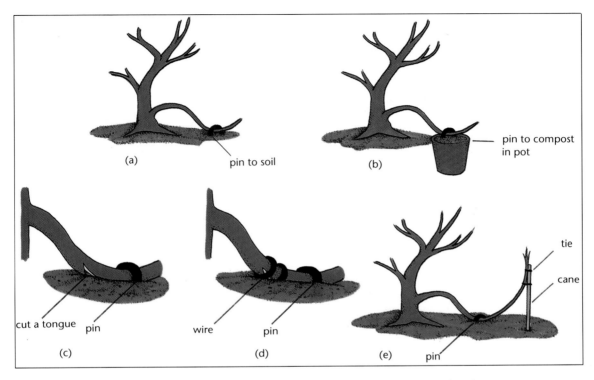

(a) pin to soil

(b) pin to compost in pot

cut a tongue pin

(c)

wire pin

(d)

tie

cane

(e) pin

Fig 37 Layering is a good way of propagating trees which are difficult to propagate from normal cuttings.

gation are that trees with a thick trunk can be produced in a short time whilst trees which would normally be too tall ('leggy') can still be used.

The first thing you need to do is to pick a suitable branch or area just above the 'leggy' section, bearing in mind the thickness of the trunk and a well-spaced network of branches. The part of the tree chosen for air-layering can be encouraged to grow in the desired shape by pruning one or two years before propagation takes place.

Make a cut half-way through the branch or at the base of your future trunk. Dust the blade of your knife with a rooting hormone, the type used for semi-ripe and hardwood cuttings. Run the blade of the knife through the cut you have just made, wiping the hormone powder from the blade into the cut.

The cut is then kept open by packing moist sphagnum moss into it. Add more moist sphagnum moss outside the cut and wrap the section of the branch in clear polythene, sealing it at both ends with tape. When the polythene is filled with a white root-growth, the air-layer can be removed from the mother tree.

Alternatively, when dealing with hard, woody, outdoor bonsai, make two cuts (one on each side of the trunk or branch) and follow the steps previously described. The important thing to remember is to keep the cuts open by packing with moss peat. Then, cover the area as previously described.

The third option is to remove two sections of bark, but maintain a central section which carries the sap-flow from the mother tree to the intended new tree.

[57]

GRAFTING

Grafting is probably the hardest form of propagation and it may take you several years to acquire such skills. When finally mastered, however, grafting will enable you to propagate trees such as crab apple (*Malus*), cherry (*Prunus*) and plum (*Prunus*). It can also give satisfying results when grafting two colours on to one branch or when trying to produce a thick trunk. The most important part of grafting is to collectively bring together all areas of cambium from the rootstock and the scion as shown in Fig 38.

To 'graft' is to form a union between two separate parts of a tree; the lower or root area being called a 'rootstock' and the top piece being called a 'scion'.

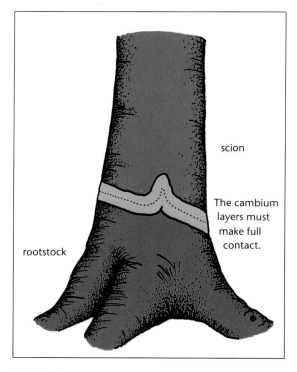

Fig 38 The marriage of the two cambium layers is the most important factor in grafting.

Rootstock Before you start to learn how to graft, you should first understand more about the rootstock. To assemble a successful graft, the rootstock and the scion must be compatible.

The following list indicates the compatible rootstock for most of the trees used for bonsai.

Tree	Recommended rootstock
Beech (*Fagus*)	*Fagus sylvatica*
Cedar (*Cedrus*)	*Cedrus deodara*
Cherry (*Prunus*)	*Prunus avium*
Crab apple (*Malus*)	*Malus sylvestris*
Hawthorn (*Crataegus*)	*Crataegus monogyna*
Juniper (*Juniperus*)	*Juniperus virginiana*
Larch (*Larix*)	*Larix decidua*
Maple (*Acer*, most types)	*Acer palmatum*
sycamore	*A. pseudoplatanus*
Norway maple	*A. platanoides*
Mountain ash (*Sorbus*)	*Sorbus aucuparia*
Pine (*Pinus*)	*Pinus thunbergii*
Rhododendron	*Rhododendron ponticum*
Spruce (*Picea*)	*Picea abies*
Spruce (*Picea*)	*Picea pungens* (blue)
Yew (*Taxus*)	*Taxus baccata*

Types of Graft

There are several ways of grafting, but I only use four to grow bonsai:

1. Whip-and-tongue.
2. Cleft graft.
3. Saddle graft.
4. Veneer graft.

Whip-and-Tongue

Dormant wood is used for this common form of grafting which is carried out between February and March, outside in a sheltered spot, or in an unheated glasshouse. First, cut into the rootstock (which should have been chosen during the previous growing season). Prepare the scion, tie the graft and apply wax.

Cleft Graft

This is a good way to produce a bonsai with a thick trunk and a network of top branches. The rootstock used for the cleft graft is much thicker than the scion or scions. Make a V-shape cut at the top of the rootstock, and wedge the scion into it. Then, wrap the graft with raffia.

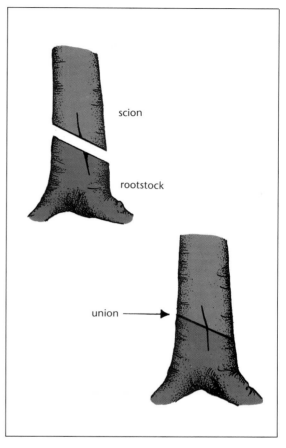

Fig 39 Whip-and-tongue can be used for grafting trees such as maples.

Raffia and Grafting Wax

Raffia is a tough, string-like material used to hold the two surfaces of rootstock and scion together firmly, but not too firmly.

Grafting wax looks like a very thick jelly. It helps to keep water out of the union and also prevents the area from drying out in windy conditions or during warm weather. The wax is heated by placing the container into hot water or by placing into a recipient with bottom heat which has been designed for the purpose. The wax then melts and, when soft, is applied to the union with a brush or the end of a chopstick.

Saddle Graft

I very seldom use this type of graft and then only to grow bonsai rhododendrons. For the saddle graft, both rootstock and scion need to be of the same thickness. Saddle grafting on rhododendrons is carried out during the winter months. Use the *Rhododendron ponticum* rootstock and place it on a warm bench, or plunge it into peat between the months of November and December with a bottom heat temperature of 21°C (70°F).

Cut the rootstock down to about 5cm (2in) and shape it (*see* Fig 41). The point to remember is that you are trying to create a small, attractive bonsai and the position of the graft and the ability to hide it at a later stage is a very important factor to take into consideration.

The same applies to the scion or part to be

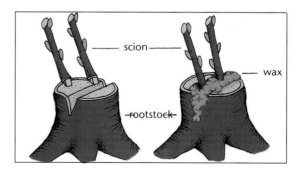

Fig 40 A cleft graft. The most important factor is to bring the cambium of the scion and rootstock into full contact. The cleft graft is ideal for forming a tree with two trunks.

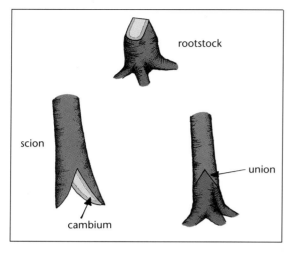

Fig 41   The saddle graft is ideal for rhododendrons.

grafted on to the rootstock. They must match to form a non-bulky union which, at a later date, will form an interesting-looking trunk. Therefore, carefully cut the scion to fit the rootstock exactly: the two cambium layers must make full contact.

Tightly hold the two parts together by tying raffia around the union.

The rootstock and scion should continue to receive bottom heat until such time as the graft has taken.

Veneer Graft

Again, bottom heat is advisable with this type of graft. Shape the end of the scion then place it into the cut made low down on the rootstock.

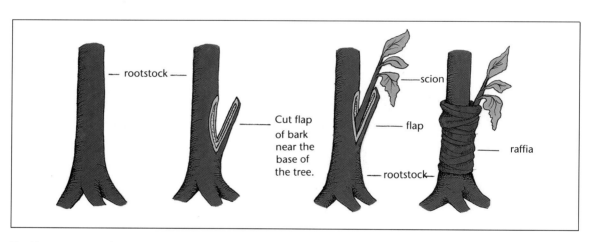

Fig 42   A veneer graft. Again, the secret is to link the two cambium layers together. The veneer graft is ideal for creating side branches.

Chapter 5

PESTS AND DISEASES

This chapter relates to those pests and diseases found in the Western hemisphere, and more especially in the UK. However, whether you live in the eastern or western part of the world, it will still take time and experience to learn to recognize attacks from pests and the colour changes and markings relating to diseases. By following the old saying 'Prevention is better than cure', a hygiene and spraying programme (organic if possible) for both pests and diseases will help to eliminate some of the most common problems and should help to keep your bonsai strong and healthy.

Government regulations differ in all parts of the world, so contact the governing bodies of your own country to find out about importing and exporting plants before attempting to do either. First, obtain a certificate of health from the country of origin and especially those outside the common market, such as Japan. Quarantine periods will differ from one country to the next, so again, check with the relevant governing bodies.

Some trees do find their way *illegally* in and out of countries. *Do not* purchase such a tree. It may look free of pests or diseases, but remember that appearances can deceive. In purchasing such a tree, you are taking the risk of either losing that particular bonsai, losing your complete bonsai collection as well as losing other plants growing under natural conditions through contamination.

WEATHER CONDITIONS

Note Weather conditions are unpredictable: the following recommendations should only be used as a guideline.

Frost

Frost mainly affects the hardy bonsai, but indoor bonsai growers might also benefit from reading through this section. Spring frost may cause more damage than the autumn frost and you should never be tempted to place your tree outside too early, especially if it has just been root-pruned.

Frost damage in the spring is caused by the moisture inside the cell's tissue turning into ice crystals in cold weather. In the autumn, when the tree enters its dormancy period, only very small amounts of moisture are available in the cell system to form these ice crystals. The trees are slowly introduced into the colder conditions of the winter months and therefore less damage is caused. However, evergreen indoor bonsai will still be at risk and will need full protection. The same applies to the deciduous indoor or cold room bonsai such as the Chinese water elm, Jacqueline elm and pomegranate, because the sap may still be conducting inside the tree. The tree should therefore be kept slightly under 10°C (50°F) to allow dormancy, but in a frost-free position.

During the spring, when there is more moisture to draw on, placement is a very important factor. Spring frosts attack at any time from the beginning of March until the begining of May and that is when buds, new shoots and juvenile foliage run the highest risk of being damaged. Most of the spring frosts are ground frosts which have a penetrating effect – more so than the air frost.

> **Frost Pocket**
> You will find frost where you would expect to find water. Therefore, never position your bonsai or bonsai area at the bottom of a slope, where water may collect and form what is known as a 'frost pocket'.

Light

Light during the growing season (summer) is the most important factor in successfully growing bonsai. This is especially important for those who grow indoor bonsai often fail to understand this point thinking that a tree will survive through a winter period with the aid of some form of artificial light source. 'Light' should not be confused with strong sunlight. Most bonsai, in fact, prefer filtered light, especially during hot sunny weather. The term light refers to colour temperature. Most garden centres sell small light meters and I would advise the indoor bonsai grower to invest in one before siting a bonsai. Bonsai which are kept in poor light conditions show signs of leggy growth on the stem between one set of leaves and the next. Leaves can also turn yellow (this may also be caused by over- or under-watering) because of lack of chlorophyll. The answer to the indoor bonsai grower's light problem during the winter months or the hardy grower during leaf pruning is a grow light. This is a special light that contains a similar light spectrum to that of daylight. Grow lights can be purchased world-wide from garden centres and some electrical stores.

Temperature

Temperature plays as important a part as light in the process of photosynthesis. Temperature controls the period of dormancy of the deciduous hardy and indoor bonsai and, if not correctly maintained, can be the cause of poor and leggy growth and dull-coloured foliage in the indoor bonsai.

When the deciduous indoor bonsai is kept at a constant temperature level throughout the year, the tree's dormancy period fails to develop, throwing the natural balance of the bonsai into confusion. Too high a temperature can be just as damaging as too low a temperature: problems such as heat canker will arise and some of the cold room bonsai, such as the olive tree, will drop their leaves.

Hardy bonsai The hardy, deciduous bonsai (including the evergreen trees) will need a temperature range of 4–20°C (39–70°F).

Fig 43 This photograph of a maple was taken during the winter months.

[62]

Fig 44   A pomegranate imported from Japan.

Indoor bonsai   The indoor bonsai are evergreen and deciduous, tropical and subtropical trees and shrubs. They will need a totally frost-free growing area with a temperature range of 15–20°C (59–70°F).

Cold-room bonsai   Evergreen and deciduous bonsai may be kept in temperatures ranging between 10–16°C (50–61°F), but the temperature should be allowed to fall to 4°C (39°F) to allow the deciduous tree to enter a dormancy period. (Again, totally frost-free conditions are necessary.)

Wind

Bonsai should always be protected from strong wind which would otherwise damage foliage, dry out the soil and also sections of the wood during dormancy. Early spring wind can damage young growth, which is then less resistant to frost. Wind-break material should be erected around the growing area, using materials such as mesh for glasshouse shading and repotting. This will filter approximately seventy per cent of the wind and is far better than a solid wall or fence which may cause wind turbulence.

HYGIENE

Clean Tools and a Tidy Area

Hygiene is a very important factor in the control of pests and diseases. Dead leaves, off-cuts from pruning, spent soil, etc., all contribute to the spread of pests and diseases. Therefore, your first priority before even attempting to grow bonsai should be to use and maintain clean, sterilized tools and working area.

Hygiene
Never compost diseased foliage or wood; always burn it and ensure that old pots and dishes are washed before being used again.

Chemical Sprays

Chemical sprays are giving way to more environmentally-friendly means of control, such as organic sprays and hand picking (removing pest, or pruning diseases areas by hand). Because of the size of the bonsai tree, hand picking pests is quite feasible.

If you do decide, however, to use chemical sprays, follow *to the letter* the instructions given by the manufacturers.

Never mix two chemicals together unless it states on the container that they are compatible and never follow one spray with another without first cleaning the container by

> **Chemicals**
> Some trees, such as the maple, will not tolerate chemical sprays. Hand picking might therefore be your only choice.

washing with clean water. Not only will mixing the wrong combination of chemicals prove toxic and dangerous to yourself, but it will also damage the foliage on your bonsai and may even cause the death of the tree. Avoid mixing too much spray and keep all chemicals away from children and pets.

Flowering and fruiting bonsai Sprays (even the organic ones) used during the flowering period can harm helpful insects such as bees. You should therefore seek advice on when to spray from your supplier before using any form of spray. As a general rule, never spray from flower bud-burst until all the flowers have gone over.

Diseases caused by Pruning

Chapter 7 deals with more advanced styles of bonsai, such as *Sabamiki* and *Jin* which involve peeled bark and exposed bare wood. These styles require extra care and attention to the problems of disease. Bare wood, even when treated, can cause die-back, canker, coral spot, mildew, and many other forms of disease, so that hygiene is very important. Clean tools should be used at all times and you should never use a tool that has entered an unhealthy tree.

Sealants used for covering bare wood are changing all the time, and it is therefore difficult to recommend any one make, but as a rule, choose the liquid form of sealant and one that contains a fungicide.

PESTS

This list covers pests found in the western

parts of the globe and should therefore only be used as a guideline.

Aphids (Aphididae)

Far too many forms of aphids exist to be included in this book. Only those which are connected directly or indirectly to bonsai growing are given in this list.

Aphids are known as sap suckers. They feed on the sap of young foliage and will not only make the foliage look unsightly, but

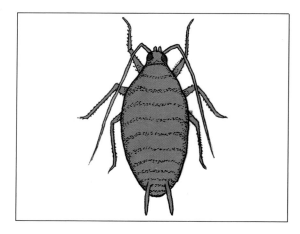

Fig 45 Aphids are sap-suckers which can transmit diseases from one tree to another.

will also weaken the entire tree if a virus is transmitted.

Aphid-infested foliage usually shows as sticky honeydew and sooty moulds.

Beech Aphid (Phyllaphis fagi)

Found on the bonsai's new foliar growth from April or May onwards, depending on the temperatures at that time of year. These aphids have a waxy-wool covering and are green to yellow in colour.

Control Use soapy water, or follow a spraying programme throughout the year, alternating between a contact and systemic insecticide.

[64]

Elder Aphid (Aphis sambuci)

With a few exceptions, not many elders are grown as bonsai, but this aphid is useful inasmuch as it helps to keep down the ant population. The elder aphid is recognized by its black colour.

Control Destroy breeding grounds such as the elder bush.

Glasshouse Aphid (Aulacorthum solani)

This aphid feeds on the young foliage of many types of indoor, cold room and outdoor bonsai during warm summers.

Control Use soapy water, or follow a spraying programme throughout the year, alternating between a contact and systemic insecticide. For maples and some forms of prunus, jet spray with soapy water once or twice a week. Smoke glasshouses to kill overwintering eggs before the start of the season.

Green Apple Aphid (Aphis pomi)

An aphid which attacks flowering and fruiting bonsai such as crab apple, cotoneaster and hawthorn. It feeds on the tree's foliage, buds and parts of the blossom, which in turn affects the fruits.

Control Use soapy water before and after flowering, or follow a spraying programme, alternating between a systemic and contact insecticide.

Lime Leaf Aphid (Eucallipterus tiliae)

Infected lime trees will show honeydew and sooty moulds. Yellow- to green-coloured aphid.

Control Use soapy water, or follow a spraying programme throughout the year, alternating between a contact and systemic insecticide.

Peach Aphid (Myzus persicae)

More troublesome than most other forms of aphids. It attacks bonsai palm trees and a wide range of other indoor bonsai. Hardy outdoor bonsai may also be attacked during a warm spring and summer. Peach aphid is yellow- to green-coloured and in some cases mixed pink-yellow to green.

Control Use soapy water, or follow a spraying programme throughout the year, alternating between a contact and systemic insecticide. Smoke glasshouses to kill overwintering eggs.

Privet Aphid (Myzus ligustri)

The privet bonsai suffers from attacks by the privet aphid, also known as the privet leaf roller, because it rolls the leaves and feeds inside of them, causing some bonsai to drop their foliage.

Control Use soapy water, or follow a spraying programme throughout the year, alternating between a contact and systemic insecticide from spring onwards.

Root Aphids (Pemphigus species)

Several different forms of aphid, varying in colour from black to white and some with a wax covering, will attack the root system of indoor and cold room bonsai. Attacks from the root aphid may cause the bonsai to wilt and die.

Control Checking the root system when the tree is repotted is advisable. If discovered, follow this procedure:

1. Remove all the compost from the root system by gently flushing with clean water.
2. Spray the entire root system with a contact insecticide.
3. Repot without root pruning in fresh compost, allowing the root system to recover for the next growing season before root pruning.

Spruce Aphid (Elatobium abietinum)

This green-coloured aphid feeds on spruce and picea, causing the foliage to turn yellow.

[65]

Control Use soapy water, or follow a spraying programme, alternating between a contact and systemic insecticide from the beginning of March.

Sycamore Aphid (Drepanosiphum platanidis)

This green and large aphid attacks maples, feeding on the buds and foliage.

Control Spray soapy water with a forceful jet twice a week. Remove dead insects by hand.

Willow Aphid (Tuberolachnus salignus)

This large brown aphid feeds on the woody section of willows.

Control Use soapy water, or follow a spraying programme from May onwards, alternating between a contact and systemic insecticide.

Woolly Aphid (Eriosoma lanigerum)

This brown aphid covered in a white wooly wax can be a serious threat to bonsai growers. It feeds on the fine twiggy branches of several types of bonsai, especially those flowering and fruiting types such as crab apple, cotoneaster and hawthorn. Branches that have been attacked may die back, or, in the case of crab apple, form a canker. *See* dieback and canker.

Control Use soapy water, or follow a spraying programme throughout the year, alternating between a contact and systemic insecticide. Remove dead insects by hand (use a cotton bud dipped in white spirit).

Capsid Bugs (Capsidae)

Apple Capsid (Plesiocoris rugicollis)

This will attack the crab apple and hawthorn. The young capsid bug may be found feeding on the new foliage and blossom. Yellow-to green-coloured.

Control Check bonsai during the winter period for signs of eggs. These are usually found hidden away in fine, twiggy parts of the bonsai. Eggs can be rubbed off by hand, using a cotton bud covered with methylated spirit. Spray a contact or systemic insecticide from spring onwards, but not during the flowering period.

Common Green Capsid (Lygocoris padulinus)

See apple capsid.

Caterpillars (Lepidoptera)

Caterpillars are the young (larvae) of moths and butterflies. The majority that attack bonsai are moth larvae and most are controlled in the same way as other insects; following a spraying programme or hand picking. As with the aphid, however, some will only attack certain types of bonsai.

Azalea Leaf Miner (Caloptilia azaleella)

This caterpillar will attack indoor azaleas, causing the foliage to drop and become unsightly. Small, yellow-to-green caterpillars can be found hiding in the leaves, which it pulls together with silk threads.

Control Hand-pick, or alternate spraying with a contact and a systemic insecticide before and after flowering, but not whilst the bonsai is in bloom.

Goat Moth (Cossus)

Mainly found on elms with thick trunks. Unlike most caterpillars that feed on the foliage of a bonsai, this juvenile and fairly large pink to red-brown caterpillar (which also attacks ash, beech, oak and many other types of bonsai) causes its damage by tunnelling into the base of the bonsai's trunk. The adult lays its eggs during the night in any crooks and crannies it may find on the bonsai's trunk between the months of June and July. When the eggs hatch, the caterpil-

lars eat their way into the trunk where they may stay for long periods, feeding on the inside of the trunk.
Control Spray a jet of contact insecticide followed by a fine mist to give a fumigating effect.

Hawthorn Webber (Scythropia crataegella)

Attacks hawthorn and cotoneaster. The first sign of this small yellow-to-brown, sometimes red, caterpillar is a fine silk webbing on the branch system from spring onwards.
Control Hand-pick, or follow a spraying programme throughout the year, alternating between a contact and systemic insecticide. Remove any cocoons found and destroy them.

Juniper Webber (Dichomeris marginella)

Junipers can be seriously affected by this caterpillar. The juniper webber is small and brown and causes unsightly brown patches which may finally lead to the death of the branch or complete tree. Foliage turning brown may also be caused by other problems, such as windscorch, but if the caterpillar is present you will find a silk webbing.
Control Hand-pick, or follow a spraying programme throughout the year, alternating between a contact and systemic insecticide.

Oak Tortrix (Tortrix viridana)

Also known as 'hanging caterpillar' because of the way it hangs from the end of branches on silk threads. This green-to-grey caterpillar damages the tree by pulling the foliage together and eating the leaves from the inside, which also makes the oak bonsai look unsightly.

Common Tortrix

Other forms of *Tortrix* may attack your bonsai tree and a good way of identifying this caterpillar is to place it on the ground and touch its head, which, if it is a tortrix, will make a backward movement.
Control Hand-pick, or follow a spraying programme throughout the year, alternating between a contact and systemic insecticide.

Pine Looper (Bupalus piniaria)

The damage is caused by this large green caterpillar eating the pine needles and causing large brown unsightly patches on the tree. The pine looper hangs on a silk thread in a similar manner to the *Tortrix*.
Control Hand-pick, or follow a spraying programme throughout the year, alternating between a contact and systemic insecticide.

Pine Shoot Moth (Rhyacionia buoliana)

This small caterpillar works its way into the buds of the bonsai pine, where it then stays during the winter months and destroys the new growth in the spring.
Control Hand-pick, or follow an alternate spraying with a contact and a systemic insecticide, carrying the programme into the later part of the autumn and early part of the winter.

Gall Mites (Eriophyidae)

These are small mites which feed on the bonsai's tissue. They cause very little damage, except for causing the bonsai grower to worry that the tree has some incurable disease.
Control Except for maples, follow a spraying programme, alternating between both contact and systemic insecticides and fungicide. The chemicals should be compatible.

[67]

Oak-Apple Gall Wasp (Biorhiza pallida)

Like the acorn gall, this wasp attacks oaks, but this time forms small ball-shaped growths from spring onwards, in which the juvenile (larvae) feed. As the gall develops, it turns red in colour.
Control Although this gall is unsightly, it does little harm to the bonsai. To remove, cut back to growing point.

Mealy Bugs (Pseudococcidae)

The mealy bug is recognized by its white-waxy covering which attacks the bonsai, weakening it and therefore rendering it unsuitable for bonsai training. Most mealy bugs are found on the bonsai's branches and trunk, but on occasions will infest the root system.
Control Mealy bugs survive best in a warm temperature, therefore ventilate to keep temperatures down. Removing by hand, using a cotton bud dipped in methylated spirit, is the best way to destroy this pest. Make sure to isolate any infected bonsai until the bonsai is completely free from the pest. Follow a spraying programme, alternating between a contact and systemic insecticide.

Mites (Acarina)

Conifer Mite (Oligonychus ununguis)

This particular mite attacks the bonsai from the beginning of the year onwards, causing its leaves to turn yellow and in some cases drop its foliage. Indoor pine and conifers can be seriously damaged by this mite.
Control Spray foliage with a fine mist containing clean water, or start your spraying programme from the end of March, alternating between a contact and systemic insecticide.

Red Spider Mites

Fruit tree (*Panonychus ulmi*) This is the main, but not the only red spider to attack your fruiting bonsai such as peach.
Control Spray with a fine mist of clean water, or follow a spraying programme using one of the chemicals for fruit red spider

> **Red Spider Mite**
> The very name automatically leads you to think along the lines of the common spider, such as might be found in the house. In fact, although mites and spiders share a distant ancestry and are both characterized by their speed of movement, they are totally different in shape.

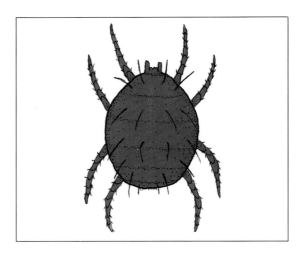

Fig 46   Red spider mites will increase in numbers during hot, dry summers.

Rhododendron Bug (Stephanitis rhododendri)

Juvenile bugs (nymphs) start feeding on the foliage from spring onwards, causing the leaves to turn yellow and brown and then finally drop off.
Control Hand-pick, or alternate spraying

[68]

with a contact and systemic insecticide from the end of March onwards, throughout the growing season.

Scale Insects (Coccidae)

Scale on Beech (Cryptococcus fagisuga)

The scale found on the beech's branches and trunk looks like a white powder, but on close examination it is also waxy. Attacks from the scale weaken the bonsai, so that it is more likely to develop a disease in the later stages.

Fig 47   Scale insects can be removed by hand.

Control   Remove by hand any over-wintering eggs found on the branches and trunk of the bonsai during the winter months. Use a cotton wool pad and surgical spirit. Follow a spraying programme, alternating between a contact and systemic insecticide.

Scale on Horse Chestnut (Pulvinaria regalis)

This does very little harm on the bonsai, but is unsightly. Other bonsai may also be attacked, among which are maple, elm and lime.

Control   *See* scale on beech.

Mussel Scale (Lepidosaphes ulmi)

Shaped like its name suggests, this brown scale attacks bonsai crab apple and cotoneaster.

Control   Remove by hand using a cotton wool pad and surgical spirit during the growing season and winter months. Make sure you follow a spraying programme, alternating between a contact and systemic insecticide.

Scale on Oleander (Aspidiotus nerii)

Affects mainly indoor, cold room and some hardy outdoor bonsai. Indoor bonsai such as acacia, azalea, ficus and palms are most affected.

Control   Hand-pick or follow a spraying programme throughout the year, using both contact and systemic insecticides. Take care when spraying in an enclosed area. Follow the same programme as for *Cryptococcus fagisuga*.

Scale on Woolly Currant (Pulvinaria ribesiae)

Known for attacking currants, but will also attack birch, hawthorn, cotoneaster and willow.

Control   Follow the same programme as for *Cryptococcus fagisuga*.

Scale on Woolly Vine (Pulvinaria vitis)

Almost the same as the woolly currant. Follow the same control procedures as for *Cryptococcus fagisuga*.

[69]

DISEASES

Canker

Affects ash, beech, crab apple, cherries and hawthorn.

Apple Canker (Nectria galligena)

Detected by a papery bark, or a cream-coloured pustule growth in the spring, red in the winter, and branches dying back close to the affected area.
Control Remove and burn infected wood. Cover pruning cuts with a sealant containing fungicide. Spray with a systemic fungicide throughout the growing season, especially in late autumn.

Ash Canker (Nectria galligena)

Ash trees which have been severely damaged by a spring frost are more prone to attacks by canker. Look out for rings in the affected areas.
Control Avoid spring and autumn frosts. Follow a spraying programme throughout the year, using a systemic fungicide. Remove branches damaged by frost, cutting back to clean wood.

Beech Bark Canker (Nectria)

Beech scale (*Cryptococcus fagisuga*) causes the damage and allows the spores of this fungus to enter.
Control Spray to control the beech scale (*see* previous page) and follow a spraying programme, using a fungicide. Remove and burn infected wood.

Coral Spot (Nectria cinnabarina)

This fungus will chiefly attack outdoor bonsai, but it is important for the indoor bonsai grower to understand a little about the disease, especially when the indoor bonsai is placed outside. Coral spot will cause die-

Fig 48   Coral spot can be fatal, therefore never leave stumps.

back and in most cases kill the tree, or cause some drastic pruning, thus altering the shape of the bonsai. In extreme cases, destroy the bonsai by burning.

Coral spot is identified by its salmon-pink coloured growths about the size of a pinhead.
Control Rules for prevention should be followed *to the letter*. Pruning is the best cure for this disease, but the cut should be made several centimetres away from the diseased areas, back into clean wood. Sometimes, the pruning may be so drastic that you might consider whether it is worth keeping the bonsai.

Damping Off

See Chapter 3, page 45.

Die-Back

Many bonsai suffer from die-back in one form or another. Die-back may be caused by fungi and bacteria, leading to forms of canker; it can also be caused by scale insects (which also help to introduce fungi into the bonsai), viruses, frost damage, strong winds and bad pruning.
Control Remove diseased branches, cutting

Prevention
1.   Hygiene is the most important factor. Never leave pruning wood lying about. Always keep a plastic bag in which to place pruning rejects, and then burn them at the first opportunity.
2.   Check for old tree stumps in the garden, close to the bonsai area. Cut, remove and burn them if found. At the same time, check all old wood for signs of the fungus (for instance, at the bottom of back doors, especially in old cottages or buildings).
3.   Always use fresh soil which is pest- and disease-free. Check your soil mixing area and board. If any signs of coral spot are found, burn your mixing board and find a replacement.
4.   When pruning, during the summer- or winter-time, make sure that the cuts are close to a joint and on an angle that allows water to run away from the pruning cut. (*See* Chapter 1, page 13).
5.   Always clean your pruning tools with methylated or surgical spirit before use. Brush all pruning cuts with a wound sealant directly after finishing the cut.
6.   Check for signs of the disease early in the year, especially in the spring. Use a systemic fungicide throughout the growing season.

back into clean wood. As soon as the diseased part has been removed, cover the wound with a sealant containing a fungicide. Never keep the prunings; burn them or place them into a plastic bag until such time as burning is convenient. Follow a spraying programme using a fungicide throughout the growing season.

Galls

These are growths and swellings found on the leaves, stems and roots of bonsai and are caused by fungi and bacteria. They may look unsightly, but do little harm to the tree, except in the case of the root gall which can weaken the tree.

Control Use a fungicide throughout your spraying programme. Change compost if root gall is found and never use old compost.

Rhododendron Gall
(Exobasidium vaccinii)
Found on the foliage as a swelling which starts with an orange-red colour and turns to white as the spores start to grow.
Control Remove by hand before the swelling turns white. This will help to stop the spread of the spores. Follow a fungicide spraying programme alternating between contact, systemic fungicide and insecticide. Make sure the chemicals are compatible.

Chapter 6

MONTH-BY-MONTH GUIDE

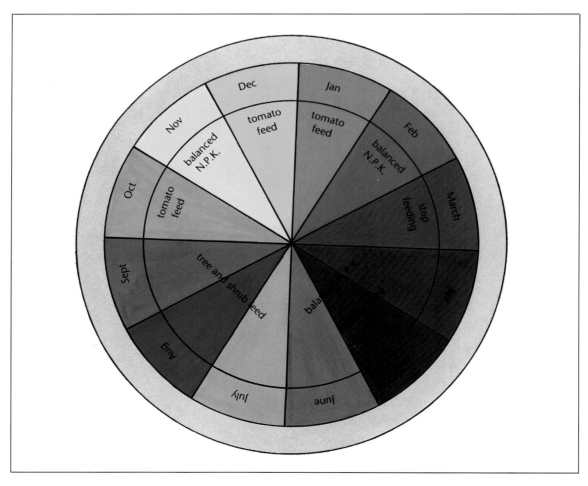

Fig 49   Feeding clock for the bonsai year.

HARDY BONSAI

January

Snow Remove snow from trees which are overwintering in the soil, or place under cover, but with as much light as possible.

Rain Never allow the root area to become waterlogged.

Watering Water to prevent the soil from drying out, never allow it to become water-logged, which could in turn freeze solid during the low temperatures.

Feeding Do not feed the tree this month, since damage can be caused to the root system by a build-up of unused fertilizers becoming toxic.

Pests Deciduous bonsai are usually pest-free except if they are being used as over-wintering host plants. Check the tree very closely for pests and remove any pest found by hand.

Diseases Look out for diseases such as rots and mould.

February

Conditions and procedures are the same as for January.

Planning for March
February is an excellent month in which to plan the coming year's root pruning. This may start from March onwards.

Pots Choose sizes, colours and shapes that will balance well with the trees that will need repotting.

Equipment Maintenance of tools and sprays that need cleaning and/or repairing.

Fig 50 A maple from the author's collection, showing well-balanced branches.

Pruning For those hardy trees kept outside without heat in a cold frame or buried in the soil, now is the time to check for frost damage. If large branch work has been affected, mark ready for pruning back to clean wood at the beginning of March. Smaller branches can be marked ready for the end of March.

Hardy seed sowing Visit your local garden centre and look through their seeds and their suppliers' catalogues for your hardy bonsai seeds.

Soil Check with your local garden centre to see when fresh supplies for making your compost will be available.

Pests Hardy bonsai are usually trouble-free at this time of year.

[73]

Diseases Wilts, die-back and frost damage may be a problem this month. (*See* Chapter 5).

March

Root pruning and repotting month. The days are beginning to lengthen, temperatures are rising and the buds will start to swell. Frost and low temperatures can still be a problem.

Forcing your tree Do not force the buds to open by using artificial heat or by leaving your tree in a glasshouse, where the day temperature will rise considerably. In such conditions, when temperatures may rise up to 21°C (70°F) or higher, and night temperatures can drop almost to zero, permanent damage and even death may occur. Ventilation therefore plays a vital part in controlling the temperature so that the tree does not suffer from rapid changes of temperature.

Snow Remove any snow from branches of trees overwintering in the soil. Place tree in sheltered area.

Rain Do not allow the root area to become waterlogged.

Wind For those trees kept outside and growing in the soil, shelter from strong winds by using hessian or plastic windbreaks.

Feeding Start feeding during the last two weeks of this month. Follow feeding programme, keep a record of when you fed your tree and the type of feed given.

Root pruning and repotting This is the major month for pruning most of your hardy bonsai (and indoor bonsai). Again, rather than setting a time, you should be governed by the movement of the buds.

After the root pruning, the four most important rules to follow are:

1. Not to overwater.
2. Not to feed for 3–4 weeks.
3. Keep out of frost.
4. Shelter from strong winds.

On no account should you force your hardy bonsai after root pruning by placing it on a warm bench. This could expose the damaged root system to a sudden change in temperature.

All large branch pruning should have been carried out by this time.

Wiring Start wiring your trees where needed. (*See* Chapter 1, page 14).

Pests and Diseases At the end of the month, start hand-picking or chemical-spraying with a systemic insecticide and fungicide. Look for signs of caterpillars.

> **Caution**
> If using chemical control, spray all maples with a systemic insecticide just before bud burst. Care should be taken with insecticidal sprays after bud burst, especially with the maple species (*see* Chapter 5, page 64).

April

Wind Keep the tree out of strong winds.

Watering Do not allow the soil to dry out.

Feeding Start feeding with a balanced N.P.K.

Pests Aphids, mealy bugs and caterpillars start to appear. Commence a spraying programme and remove any pest found by hand. Avoid spraying close to maples, which may cause marking on the foliage; spray maples with clean soapy water.

Start flow.

End flow before can runs out.

Fig 51   Move the watering-can backwards and forwards over the seed tray to avoid puddling.

May

Frost   Night frost can still be a problem. The tree should now be in a period of active growth. Keep a check on top and side growth.

Rain   If heavy rainfall this month, tilt the bonsai pot.

Watering   Check the water level daily; do not let the soil dry out and do not water when the sun's rays are beating strongly down on the foliage. Try to water before 10 a.m. or after 5 p.m. If heavy rainfall this month, tilt the pot to one side to drain excess water.

Feeding   Use a tomato feed for flowering and fruiting trees, and a general balanced N.P.K. feed on all others.

June

Leaf pruning time for deciduous trees (*see* Chapter 7.

Watering   As for May.

Feeding   As for May.

July

Semi-ripe cuttings (*see* Chapter 4).

Watering   As for May.

Feeding   As for May.

August

Start cutting down on the nitrogen feeds.

Watering   As for May.

Feeding   Less nitrogen.

September

Check for insects looking for places in which to overwinter. Prune pines (*see* Chapter 7).

Watering   As for May.

Feeding   Stop feeding at the end of the month.

October

Get trees ready for their winter position.

[75]

Wind   When required, shelter trees from strong winds.

Watering   As for May.

Feeding   Stop feeding.

November and December

Trees should be in their winter position. Check for overwintering pests.

Watering   As for May.

Feeding   As for May.

INDOOR BONSAI

January

As outdoor temperatures drop, indoor temperatures are raised by switching on and turning up the central heating. Remember, however, that a constant temperature should be maintained at all times (*see* Chapter 9). The warm air which results from gas central heating presents itself as the frist major problem. Spray the bonsai with a mist gun to relieve from a dry atmosphere. The leaves will be affected by dust, which in turn can prevent some of the light from reaching the leaves.

Position   Give your tree as much light as possible. Natural light is most beneficial, even for those bonsai grown under grow lights. As a rough guideline, avoid positioning your tree by a window early in the morning (6 a.m.) and after 7 p.m. You may place the tree on a window-sill with a radiator below, provided that the tree is not resting in direct heat and the temperature does not reach a higher level than that recommended for the particular variety of tree. Rotate the tree each day, as this will allow for balanced growth on front, back and sides.

Note   Never place your tree on top of the television.

Watering/misting   Use rainwater if possible, or boiled tap water that has been left to stand for over twenty-four hours. Water from the top of the pot; do not leave the pot to stand in water. Spray the foliage of the bonsai with a fine mist spray to overcome the problem of a dry atmosphere.

Humidity Trays
These can be used, provided that you follow the all-important rule of never allowing the base of the pot to be submerged in water for long periods of time.

Feeding   Continue to follow a feeding programme during this month.

Pests   Keep a check on your bonsai for pests, looking along the top and underside of the leaves as well as in the crowded areas of the branch work. As far as possible, remove any pest found by hand.

Diseases   Mainly trouble-free this time of year, although there may be problems caused by:

1.   Bad pruning: die-back and rots.
2.   Lack of light: black growing tips.
3.   Poor ventilation: general unhealthy look.
4.   Temperature/watering: mildews, wilting and rots.
5.   Overfeeding: wilting, or too much sappy growth.

February

The month of February is similar to January for temperature and light conditions.

[76]

Watering   Keep a check on watering and spray over the foliage in dry atmospheres (in gas central-heated atmospheres especially).

Feeding   Stop feeding.

Equipment   Maintenance of pruning tools that need cleaning and/or repairing.

Root pruning and repotting   At this time of year, everybody is starting to think of repotting their tree or trees and suppliers of pots may find it hard to keep up with the demand. I would therefore suggest purchasing your pots at the earliest opportunity, otherwise you may be disappointed in finding the right pot at the right time. It is advisable (if root pruning and repotting) to choose a pot either the same size or slightly larger than the current one and never to overpot (using a pot several times larger than the root ball).

Seeds   Start looking for suppliers of indoor bonsai seed, ready to start sowing at the end of the month.

Compost   Do not mix your compost until the end of this month, but check with your garden centre when fresh supplies of materials will be arriving.

Pests and diseases   Check for pest and remove by hand if possible, otherwise spray (*see* Chapter 5).

March

This is probably the busiest month of the year, with root pruning and repotting first on the list.

Watering   As a general rule, start to increase the watering, but at the same time do not overwater, especially those trees which have been root-pruned. Do not stand the pot in water for long periods. Continue to spray over the foliage if a humidity tray is not used. As far as possible use rain water, or boiled tap water that has been left to stand for over twenty-four hours.

Feeding   Start to use a balanced N.P.K. feed plus trace elements. Make sure it is of the foliar-feed type if the tree has been root-pruned.

Seed sowing   If this has not already been done, March is a good time to start (*see* Chapter 3).

Cuttings   Provided you have some form of bottom heat, such as a propagator (with a thermostat control), start taking softwood cuttings (*see* Chapter 4).

Fig 52   A selection of bonsai pots.

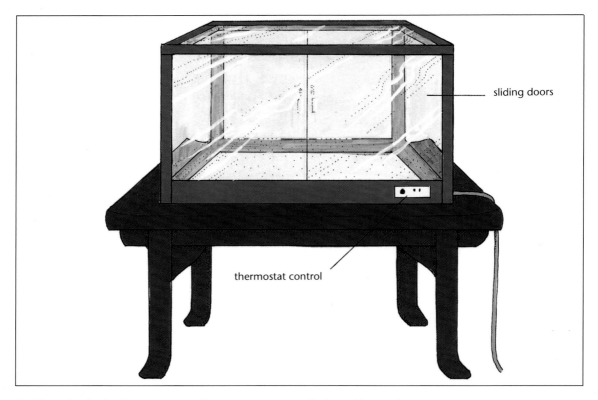

sliding doors

thermostat control

Fig 53   A simple electric propagator will give you more control when taking cuttings.

Pests and diseases   Aphids and red spider mites will start to appear from this month onward.

April

This month, most of your indoor trees should start producing plenty of new growth. The bonsai has just spent several months having to contend with fluctuations in light and temperatures, therefore, even though you should keep the tree under control, allow it to take a rest and spread its branches this month.

Position   Give the bonsai as much light as posible, but not direct sunlight. Trees placed close to windows, should be removed and positioned inside the room away from the window at night, when temperatures may still drop below 0°C (32°F).

Place the tree outside on warm sunny days, but try to avoid too much temperature change.

Frost   In most cases, frost will not affect the indoor bonsai (except if the tree is placed too close to the window at night). I would still advise you to read through the section on frost in Chapter 5.

Watering   An increase in the watering is a normal practice at this time of year.

Feeding   Continue to feed with a balanced fertilizer.

Propagation Continue to take softwood cuttings.

Pests Most of the troublesome pests such as aphids, red spider mites and caterpillars start feeding and breeding at this time of year, especially on warm sunny days. Remove pests by hand as far as possible, but at the same time stick to a preventive spraying programme.

Diseases Keep checking seeds for signs of damping off disease. Other problems such as die-back (caused by frost or previous bad pruning) should be removed and the wound covered with a sealant containing a fungicide.

Fig 54 The pomegranate is suitable for indoor growing.

May

Position On warm sunny days it will help if the bonsai can be placed outside.

Watering As for April.

Feeding As for April.

Pests and Diseases Hand-pick or follow a spraying programme throughout the year.

June

Position As for May, but on very warm nights you have the option of placing the semi-cold-room bonsai outside.

Watering As for April.

Feeding Change from the balanced feed of 7N:7P:7K: to a feed lower in nitrogen (N), but higher in phosphate (P) and potash (K). This will help to control and slow down the top growth, but will at the same time benefit the root system of those flowering bonsai as well as strengthen the new sappy growth.

Propagation Semi-ripe cuttings can be taken this month, (*see* Chapter 4). One advantage of semi-ripe cuttings is that in most cases they can do away with bottom heat.

Pests and diseases Hand-pick or follow a spraying programme throughout the year.

July

This month is basically the same as June, but extra care should be given to pests.

Placement As for June.

Watering As for April.

[79]

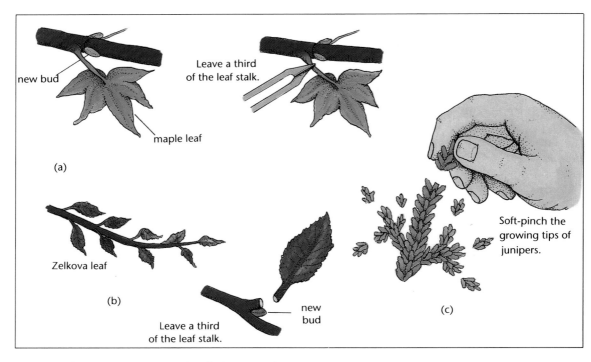

new bud

Leave a third
of the leaf stalk.

maple leaf

(a)

Zelkova leaf

(b)

Leave a third
of the leaf stalk.

new
bud

Soft-pinch the
growing tips of
junipers.

(c)

Fig 55 Leaf pruning. Never use tools to leaf-prune junipers.

Feeding As for June.

Pests and diseases Hand-pick or follow a spraying programme throughout the year, but pay extra attention to pests such as aphids and red spider mites.

August

This month generally marks the end of the summer for the indoor bonsai: temperatures may start to fall at night, as may the day temperatures towards the end of the month. It therefore becomes too risky to place the indoor bonsai outside.

Watering Keep a check on watering, which can be one of the most important factors at this time of year. A good balance between wet and dry is essential. Do not overwater.

Feeding August is a delicate month for the bonsai and, like watering, feeding is particularly important. Therefore, stick to a feeding programme and do not become tempted to overfeed. At the end of August, you can start to alternate between a feed low in nitrogen one month, and a tomato feed the next.

Pests and diseases Hand-pick, or stick to a spraying programme. For those bonsai which have been placed outside, look for moths and other pests starting to find over-wintering positions.

September

As with the month of August, temperatures can become unpredictable and it is therefore too risky to place your indoor bonsai outside. As the month draws to a close, keep checking trees that have been placed outside for pests which are either looking for a winter position or a host plant in warmer conditions. Again, light and temperature will upset the tree's time-clock, so follow the advice set out for August when it comes to watering and feed.

Position   As much light as possible, but not direct sunlight. Keep away from direct heat such as cookers and television sets. If the tree is placed in a window with a radiator below, allow at least a one metre distance.

Watering   As for August.

Feeding   As for August.

Pests and diseases   As for August.

October

Autumn frosts and low temperatures should be the main concern for those indoor bonsai kept either in a conservatory or close to a window. For the conservatory, it would be advisable to apply some form of heat so as to control the inside temperature and keep off the frost. Those bonsai kept close to a window should be moved away from the window into a more central position in the room. Again, allow the tree to get accustomed to the fluctuations of light and temperature.

Watering   As for August.

Feeding   As for August.

Pruning   Do not prune any tree that appears unwell or that has not yet adjusted to the change over to winter light and temperature. For those bonsai which have acclimatized, continue to prune new unwanted growth.

Wiring   Remove wire placed on to the tree earlier in the year (*see* Chapter 2, page 14).

Pests and diseases   Hand-pick, or follow a spraying programme throughout the year.

November

Basically the same as October, but your tree should have acclimatized itself to the indoor conditions. If not, then try moving to a lighter or shadier spot, whichever the case may be, or a cooler or warmer position.

Watering   As for August.

Feeding   As for August.

Pests and diseases   As for October.

December

Watering   As for August.

Feeding   As for August.

Pruning   Continue to remove new, unwanted growth.

Pests and diseases   Hand-pick or follow a spraying programme throughout the year.

Chapter 7

ADVANCED TECHNIQUES

Chapter 1 tackled the basics of root pruning, maintenance and simple styling to help the beginner through the first two to three years of bonsai training. This chapter takes it a stage further and explains some of the finer points of bonsai, including some traditional Japanese terms.

Some people term bonsai a 'living art form'. In this they may be right, and the creation of some beautiful trees would seem to justify that statement. However, I personally find it very hard to accept that a living plant should be treated in the same way as an inert medium such as stone or clay and cannot agree that style should come before

Fig 56   This imported juniper has been soft-pinched to produce neat pads.

Fig 57   The *Jin* technique has been used on this needle juniper, hence the white wood showing instead of the bark.

the health of the plant. For that reason, I am no great fan of practices which involve breaking branches to form the correct line of an angle, leaving untreated sections of wood or creating large hollows. However, these practices will be shown in this book, since they form a recognized part of the art of bonsai.

There is no reason why each bonsai grower cannot look into or even try some of

Tools

Larger tools are needed in the advanced stage of bonsai, as trees tend to be larger in size. If you collect from the wild, which is likely, you will need spades, picks, etc. Chain saws are also common used in bonsai. As long as these are in good working order and well maintained; as long as you wear protective clothing and face protection, then there should not be any serious problems.

To neglect the use of protective clothing is not only asking for trouble, but is also against the law. Therefore, if you do intend to use a chain saw, I would suggest that a course run by trained people, such as the Forestry Commission or other such governing bodies, should be attended.

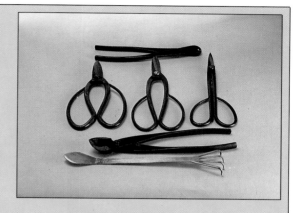

Fig 58   Some basic bonsai tools.

the practices suggested in this chapter, but I would advise starting with some basic *Jins* first before attempting more difficult styles.

The first part of this chapter particularly relates to those growers who have gone through the first two or three years of bonsai, working with small nursery stock, and are now prepared to direct their efforts towards the specimen tree range, working from soil-grown or large nursery stock. Alternatively, they are looking to reduce in size larger trees, thus saving many years of growing and producing a tree with a thick trunk, which is not always obvious when growing from seeds or cuttings. These growers are looking to acquire a collection of specimen trees in a relatively short space of time.

There are three ways of finding starting material. One is to collect specimens from the wild, the second is by cultivated methods, and the third is by purchasing large specimen trees from a tree nursery.

COLLECTING FROM THE WILD

Trees of all sizes can be collected from the wild, but in this chapter we are looking at the larger end of the scale. The first thing to remember when collecting is to get permission to do so. Bonsai clubs organize 'digging' trips, sometimes on sites which are being reclaimed by a builder, etc. Gravel pits and stone quarries are the ideal places for such digs, as are mountains and cliff faces, but extreme care should be taken in both cases.

Tools

You will need a well-shaped spade, a hand trowel, a small handsaw, a knife, pruning clippers and plastic bags in which to wrap the root system of the tree, to stop it from drying out. (The root system can in some cases dry out in a matter of minutes on a windy or hot day.)

Collecting Time

The time of year will play an important part in collecting from the wild. Early spring or late autumn are best and you should avoid collecting when the tree is in full leaf or, in the case of conifers, showing strong growth. This is the time when the sap is in full flow and the tree relies on a healthy root system to maintain it.

[83]

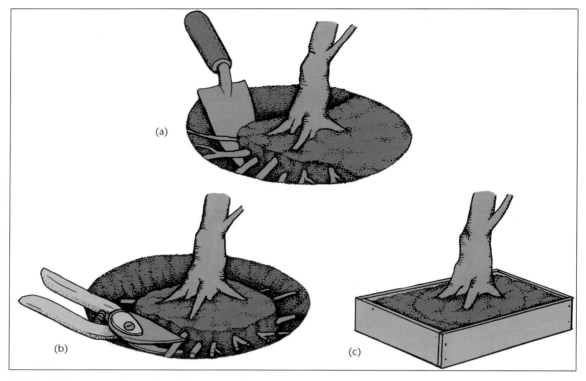

Fig 59   Collecting trees from the wild. (a) Use a sharp spade to go all the way round the tree.
(b) Cut roots. Lift without damage to roots.(c) Place the tree in a training box.

Height and Size

The ideal height when collecting from the wild is around a metre (3 feet), although you do not need to stick to it rigidly. Some trees are collected at 2–3 metres in height (6.5–10 feet). The major problem with the larger tree is the size of the root ball. In most cases, when trying to remove a large tree, the best part of the root system (the fine root hairs) is left in the soil. Therefore, a tree around a metre in height found growing in a shallow, sandy, gravel soil is your best choice.

In some cases, you may have to prune some of the branch work to make the tree easier to handle. If this is the case, then follow the normal practice of pruning back to buds or growing points and covering the cut to avoid disease.

Method

Tie a piece of string about a metre in length to the base of the trunk and then, by pulling the string tightly to its full length, create a circle all the way round the outside of the tree. Take a sharp spade and push it vertically and as deeply as possible along the edge of the circle and continue until you have gone all the way round; then move back half a metre (1.5 feet) again, pushing the spade into the soil as deeply as possible until you have completed a full circle. Then, remove the soil in between the two cuts you have made until you have formed a trench. (The trench will enable you to push your spade under the root system of the tree and at the same time cut any tap root anchoring the tree into the subsoil.)

[84]

Then, as far as possible, try to lift the tree with its full root system without losing any of the soil around the root. Quickly cover the roots with a large plastic bag to stop them from drying out; do not add water to the soil at this stage. As soon as you arrive home, place the tree into a large training box, in most cases made out of wood; do not root-prune if possible.

Over the next year, the main aim is to keep the tree in a healthy condition, so that bonsai training should be kept to a minimum: light pruning to maintain a basic shape, feeding and pest and disease control, as normal. In the second year, reduce the root system by one-third and start a normal training programme incorporating pruning and wiring.

CULTIVATED TREES

The difference between a cultivated tree and a wild tree is that the cultivated tree receives bonsai training whilst growing in the soil and the difference between a soil-grown tree and a potted tree is that the soil-grown tree will grow faster than if placed in a pot.

Method

In this practice, a tree should have been chosen (usually from nursery stock which has not yet reached specimen standard) for bonsai material, and allowed to grow in the soil as it would under normal circumstances in the open, except that in most cases it is root-pruned or has the roots cut by pushing a sharp spade into the soil every two to three years to encourage a fibrous root growth. Special growing areas can be created, which have good drainage and a built-up, balanced soil. Occasionally, slabs can also be placed several centimetres under the surface of the soil to stop the root system from penetrating too deep into the subsoil.

NURSERY SPECIMENS

You may be able to find a classic specimen which only needs slight pruning and root pruning, but the only place in which you are liable to find such a tree without paying the high bonsai nursery prices is in a nursery that specializes solely in growing trees and shrubs. In general, this type of nursery deals mainly with the wholesale trade, but bonsai clubs and individuals are on occasions allowed in for a visit and can purchase such trees.

TRAINING

Root Pruning

For root pruning, follow the method set out in Chapter 1, except that you carry it out every two to four years and in some cases at even longer intervals. However, adding fresh soil to the old soil is extremely beneficial.

Sections of the Tree
A tree can be broken down into four sections:

1. The exposed root surface roots (Nebari)
2. The lower section of the trunk (Tachiagari)
3. The branch system (Yaku-eda)
   First branch system (Ichi-no-eda)
   Second branch system (Ni-no-eda)
   Third branch system (San-no-eda)
   Clinging branch (Kuitsuki-eda)
   Counterbalancing branch (Uke-eda)
   Drooping or cascade branch (Ochi-eda)
4. The top or apex of the tree (Jushin)

To this list can also be added the front of the tree (Omote) and the back of the tree (Ura).

[85]

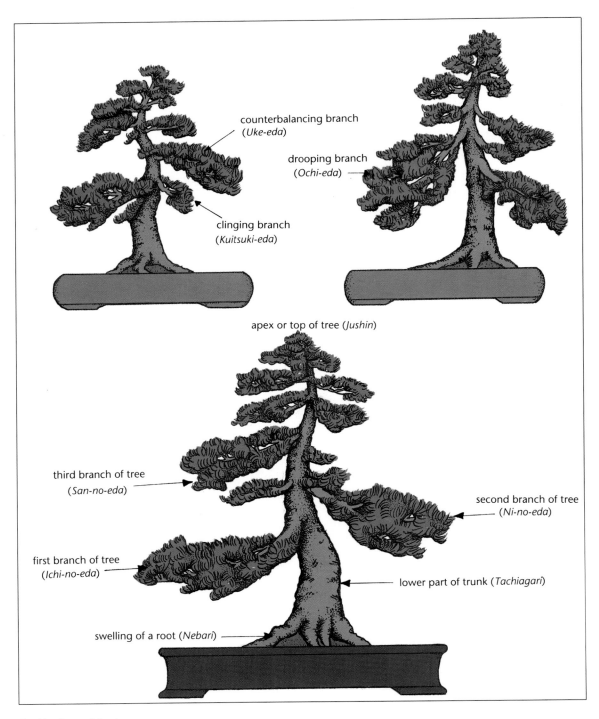

counterbalancing branch (*Uke-eda*)

drooping branch (*Ochi-eda*)

clinging branch (*Kuitsuki-eda*)

apex or top of tree (*Jushin*)

third branch of tree (*San-no-eda*)

second branch of tree (*Ni-no-eda*)

first branch of tree (*Ichi-no-eda*)

lower part of trunk (*Tachiagari*)

swelling of a root (*Nebari*)

Fig 60   Parts of the tree.

Forming Pads

Chapter 1 covered basic pruning and showed how to produce the main framework of the tree's trunk or trunks and the side and sublateral branches. In this section, we turn our attention to how to produce the pads on the main side and sublateral branches.

Upward Growth

All pads are produced on the top of the branch, even when the branch is cascading downwards; therefore, all growth that is growing downwards or on the underside of the branch should be removed. As the top growth develops, clean an area 3–5cm (1–2in) long between the main branch and the pad of all growth.

This woody section serves to give the pad a 'raised' aspect, so that it looks as if the pad

were standing on legs. As the woody section thickens, the pad stands out even more, and as the number of pads created in this manner increases, a 'cloud formation' aspect is created.

The top growth of the pad is then controlled by removing new growth which extends beyond the boundary of the pad (*see below*).

Exposed Roots (Neagari)

Exposing the roots is a matter of personal choice and it is one which I myself prefer to follow, especially in the case of surface roots. Not only do exposed roots add an aged appearance to the tree, but they are also ideal for creating many artistic shapes and forms and thus enhance the tree's beauty.

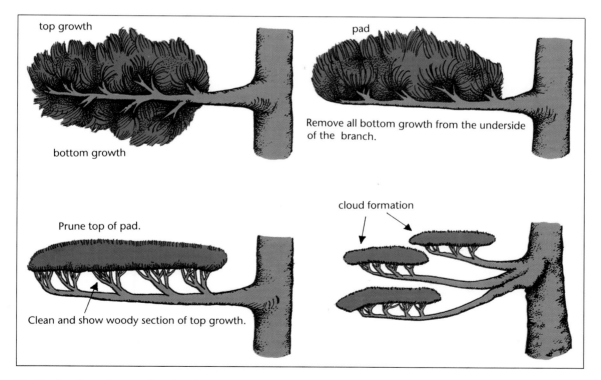

Fig 61   Pruning to form pads and multiple pads.

Grafting Roots

When collecting material for both the *Neagari* and *Sekijoju* styles, you should always look for a tree in which the base of the trunk divides off into thick woody roots. However, this is not always possible, in which case root grafting can be used.

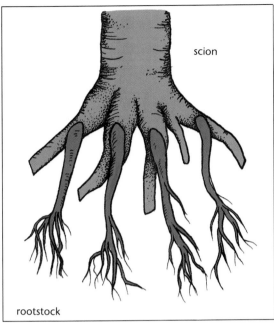

scion

rootstock

Fig 63   Root grafting is ideal for producing trees over rock.

Root grafting is normally carried out during late March/April and early May. Both sections of trunk and roots should be in good health and the roots should contain as many fine root hairs as possible. When collecting the roots, never allow them to dry out, so a hand mist-sprayer and a plastic bag are essential tools. Preventing moisture-loss around the grafted sections once the graft is completed is a very important factor in the success of the graft, but at the same time the sections should never be allowed to hold water or become waterlogged.

Fig 62   Trident maple grown over rock.

Moisture-Loss Prevention
There are several ways in which you can prevent the roots from drying out once grafted. You can use grafting wax at the time of grafting; you can cover the complete section in clean fresh soil; or you can cover the roots with tin foil.

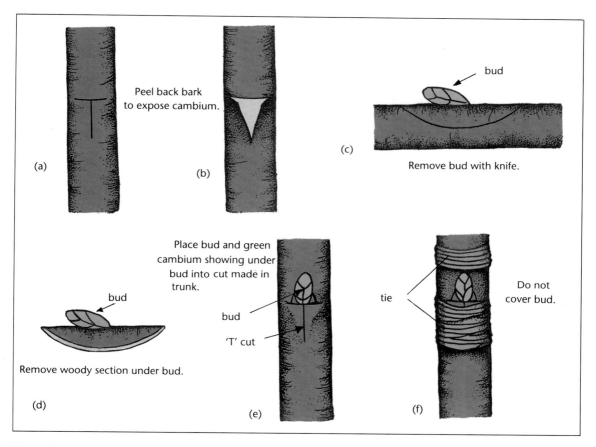

Figs 64 (a)–(f)   Budding is an ideal way to start growth from bare trunks.

Budding

The art of budding can be mastered fairly quickly and is very useful for creating side branches on long bare trunks which would otherwise have been used for the *Literati* or *Bunjingi* styles (trees with long, exposed trunks barring all growth except at the top of the tree). The best time to carry out budding is between the summer months (*see* above).

Leaf Pruning

Leaf pruning is a technique carried out on deciduous trees and some trees, such as the Japanese maple, will respond well, whilst others, such as the crab apple, do not respond as well. The best time for leaf pruning is June, preferably during a warm, sunny period. This is because you will need to produce a second set of leaves within two to three weeks if you want to keep the tree in good health; therefore, before going into the technique of leaf pruning, we need to look at and understand the conditions, and how to create those conditions, needed to produce a leaf in this space of time.

The Leaf

Foliage serves several functions. It keeps the tree cool; the wind crossing the leaves acts as

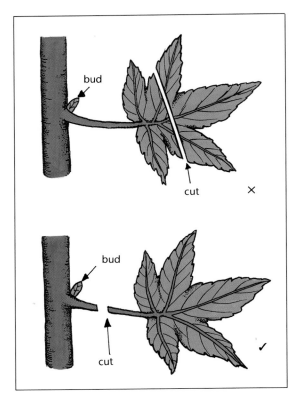

Fig 65   The correct way of removing a leaf (leaf pruning).

a pump, pulling moisture up from the root system and out through the foliage; it helps to feed the plant by producing sugar and starches through the photosynthesis process. All these factors are affected when we remove the leaves.

Photosynthesis This is the production of sugar and starches which are essential to the health of the tree and the factors which govern or control photosynthesis will stop when the leaves are removed:

1.   Chlorophyll. The leaves play a major part in the production of chlorophyll. However, other green sections will still continue to photosynthesize during the growing season when the leaves are removed.

Therefore, chlorophyll will still be present in the tree, but in smaller amounts.

2.   Light (both sunlight and artificial lighting with a colour temperature close to that of natural light). Light is a very important factor and should be provided at all times. This does not mean, however, that the tree should be placed into the baking hot sun. This would affect the level of moisture required for photosynthesis, which would in turn affect the small green sections of the tree. In addition, the tree would overheat because moisture would not be naturally lost through the foliage which generally keeps the tree cool. Weather conditions may be such that the light is too poor during the month of June, and therefore artificial lighting in the shape of a grow-light bulb should be used.

3.   Moisture. The constant moisture around the soil particle helps to keep the cells in the tree turgid. However, there needs to be a continuous movement of fresh moisture from the soil particle into the cell or root hair, and on up through other cell systems to the leaves. During the winter, the tree closes down its sap flow, so that the loss of foliage is not so important. However, when the tree is in full growth, the loss of foliage will also mean a reduction in the amount of moisture that is distributed. Watering at the time of leaf pruning should be reduced, but only by small amounts. Never allow the moisture level to drop to such an extent that the soil dries out.

4.   Carbon dioxide (CO_2) is found in the atmosphere, so good ventilation is important.

5.   Temperature. A temperature ranging between 10–18°C (50–64°F) should be maintained at all times.

Consequently, leaf pruning can take place during June provided that the right conditions are available. During cold, cloudy and windy June days, leaf pruning should be carried out in a glasshouse with a controlled temperature, good ventilation and adequate artificial lighting.

Stage One

Only prune those trees which are in good health and free from pests. The tree should be fed with a balanced soil feed two weeks before leaf pruning and one week before with a foliage feed.

Note Never overfeed the tree before removing the leaves, otherwise nutrients will remain clogged around the soil particles and become toxic because of the lack of pump action which would, under normal conditions, use the nutrients quickly.

Stage Two

Remove the leaf (*see* Fig 65), leaving about one-third of the leaf stalk.

Aftercare

Place the tree outside in good weather conditions (but away from strong winds) or, in a glasshouse when weather conditions are poor. In about two to three weeks you should see the remaining stalk fall off and a new leaf starting to grow.

PINES

The bonsai pine tree can be a very specialized subject, and one to which you could devote a complete lifetime, as is the case with a few Japanese bonsai growers. Most growers, including the experienced ones, will find the control of the needle size and the maintenance of the tree's health at the same time very difficult to achieve.

Grafted Pines

One of the most commonly known pines outside Japan is the white pine (*Pinus parviflora*) and in most cases the rootstock of

Bonsai Styles Used for the Pine Tree

Chokkan Formal upright or straight-trunk style.
Moyogi Curving or informal upright trunk.
Shakan Leaning or slanting trunk.
Bankan Twisted trunk, coiled almost like a spring.
So-kan Double trunk which divides close to the base of the trunk.
San-kan Triple trunk.
Go-kan Five trunks.
Kabudachi Multiple trunk – single tree at the base, splitting into several trunks to form a group.
Han-kengai Semi-cascade.
Kengai Cascade.
Neagari Exposed root system.
Ishitsuki Tree or trees planted on a rock.

Fig 66 The white tape on the bark marks the union of the graft between the white and black pine.

the black pine (*Pinus thunbergii*) is used for the white pine. This practice is unlike that used for most deciduous trees, which grow on their own roots with the exception of maple trees, which also tend to be grafted (*see* Chapter 4, page 58).

Soil

The soil for the pine tree should contain mycorrhizae (fungal threads) which grow inside the cortical cells or, in some cases, closely pressed to the roots, close to the surface. The close association between root and fungus could therefore be classed as symbiotic. The mycorrhiza or fungus provides a supply of nitrogen, which is then taken up by the tree through its root system, once the fungus has broken the nitrogen into soluble organic compounds.

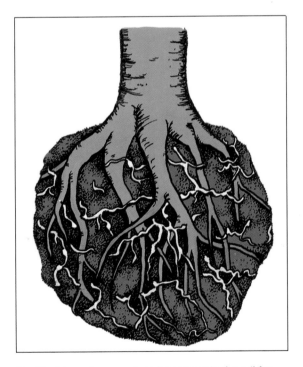

Fig 67 Mycorrhyza needs to be present in the soil for the pine tree to produce healthy growth.

To encourage the mycorrhiza, the pine tree will need a soil which contains a balanced quantity of decaying matter, such as beech leaves, hawthorn leaves and pine and larch needles.

However, never use such organic matter until it has broken down, which in most cases will take three to six months: to use untreated organic matter would burn the root system and cause the death of the tree.

Composition of the soil
*   10% Original soil containing mycorrhiza,
*   40% John Innes Code 1,
*   15% Coarse sand and grit and
*   35% well-rotted organic matter (beech, hawthorn, pine or larch needles) or coconut fibres.

Light, Water and Temperature

The light, water and temperature factors are just as important as the compositon of the soil. The pine tree not only needs soluble nitrogen, but also a carbohydrate supply. Carbohydrate is provided by photosynthesis. The process takes place in the needles (which are, in fact, modified leaves) and other green sections of the tree (*see* page 90).

Japanese Red Pine (Pinus densiflora)
Watering Regular watering during the summer months is needed. The soil should have good drainage.

Feeding Feed once during the months of April, May, June, September and October. The October feed should have a low nitrogen content.

Wiring December–March.

[92]

> **Nitrogen**
> As you reach the end of the year (September–December), less nitrogen should be used in the feed. A tomato feed or a fertilizer such as might be used for flowering or fruiting plants are ideal.

Japanese White Pine (Pinus parviflora)

Watering Little but regular watering throughout the summer. Never allow the soil to dry out completely.

Feeding Feed once during the months of April, May, June, September and October.

The October feed should have a low nitrogen content.

Wiring October–March.

Japanese Black Pine (Pinus thunbergii)

Watering Little but regular watering throughout the summer. Never allow the soil to dry out completely.

Feeding Feed once during the months of April, May, June and October. The October feed should have a low nitrogen content.

Wiring December–February.

A Guide to Pine Trees

Pinus albicaulis	
P. albicaulis 'Nana' (Nobles Dwarf)	Small, shrubby pine
Pinus armandii (Armand's pine)	Droopy or weeping pine
Pinus densiflora (Japanese red pine)	
P. densiflora 'Oculus Draconis' (dragon-eye pine)	Slow-growing pine
P. densiflora 'Pendula'	Dwarf weeping pine
P. densiflora 'Umbraculifera'	Small, slow-growing pine
Pinus koraiensis (Korean pine)	
P. koraiensis 'Winton'	Slow-growing pine
Pinus leucodermis 'Pygmy' (Bosnian pine)	Small, slow-growing, dense pine
Pinus monticola (Western white pine)	Can be grown in a weeping style
Pinus mugo (mountain pine)	Dense, slow-growing pine
P. mugo 'Gnom'	
P. mugo 'Mops'	Slow-growing pine
P. mugo 'Pumilio'	
Pinus nigra (Austrian pine)	
P. nigra 'Pygmaea'	Small, slow-growing pine
Pinus palustris (Southern pitch pine)	Slow-growing pine
Pinus parviflora (Japanese white pine)	Slow-growing pine
P. parviflora 'Adcock's Dwarf'	Slow-growing, compact pine
P. parviflora 'Brevifolia'	
P. parviflora 'Glauca'	
Pinus rigida (Northern pitch pine)	
Pinus strobus 'Nana'	Small, dense pine
P. strobus 'Nivea'	Slow-growing pine
P. strobus 'Prostrata'	
Pinus sylvestris (Scots pine)	
P. sylvestris 'Aurea'	Slow-growing pine
P. sylvestris 'Beuvronensis'	
P. sylvestris 'Doone Valley'	Small, dense pine
P. sylvestris 'Nana'	Small, bushy pine
P. sylvestris 'Watereri'	Small, slow-growing pine
Pinus thunbergii (black pine)	
P. thunbergii 'Oculus-draconis'	
Pinus uncinata 'Nana'	Dense, drooping pine

Needle Size

When growing bonsai pines, one of the hardest tasks is to reduce the size of the needles, so as to keep them in proportion with the rest of the tree. The white pine, red pine and black pine trees have been tried and tested by the Japanese for a number of years, but why not try to grow other varieties? The list on the previous page should help you to find a suitable pine.

Needle Length
Pinus banksiana (Jack pine)   76mm (3in)
Pinus canbra (Swiss pine)   76–127mm
    (3–5in)
Pinus koriensis (Korean pine)   76–127mm
    (3–5in)
Pinus strobus (Eastern white pine)
    76–127mm (3–5in)
Pinus sylvestris (Scotch pine)   76mm (3in)

Growing pine trees as bonsai requires much patience and effort. In addition, different training patterns are followed according to the pine tree chosen, i.e., whether it is a black pine (*Pinus thunbergii*), a white pine (*Pinus parviflora*) or a red pine (*Pinus densiflora*).

Take the black pine, for example. Although it is used as the rootstock for the white pine, the black pine can also be treated as an individual tree in its own right and trained in a variety of styles, such as the informal upright (*Moyogi*), cascade (*Kengai*) or semi-cascade (*Han-kengai*).

The bark of the black pine is rough, which helps to make it look deceptively older than it is. However, one disadvantage is the long needles which, if left unattended, will look out of proportion with the tree.

Pruning of the Japanese Black Pine

This can be broken down into two sections:

1.   The normal pruning of branches.
2.   The shaping of the pads and trimming of the needles, which is based on a system of renewal pruning.

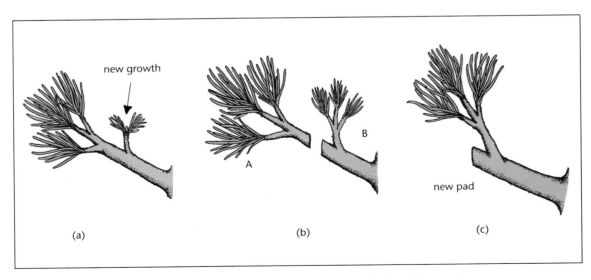

Figs 68 (a), (b) and (c)   Renewal pruning is one way of producing small pads of needle growth.

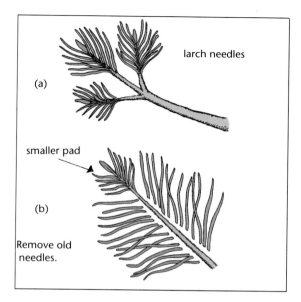

(a) larch needles

smaller pad

(b)

Remove old needles.

Fig 69   Removing older needles will give the illusion of shorter needle growth.

Note Renewal pruning in this context should not be confused with renewal prun-

ing for other trees, such as flowering or fruiting bonsai.

Branch and General Renewal Pruning

When, for example, a cluster or pad of buds and needles has grown out of shape (call this pad 'A'), a growing point as close as possible to pad A, such as a bud, can be activated by directing the sap flow to that growing point several months in advance. That point then forms into young main and lateral growth, forming pad 'B'. Pad A is then removed by cutting back to the growing point of pad B. Not only is the shape and size of the tree maintained, but it also gains a shorter needle system.

Removing Needles

This practice is known in Japan as 'old-leaf cutting'. This is where older needles are removed as shown in Fig 69. This will make the needle pads look smaller and force new growth.

The Yearly Trimming Clock	
March	Point 'A' (*see* Fig 70) shows a shoot with needles and a terminal bud (known as a 'candle'). As the bud starts to open, stop the growth by pinching. The sap flow will then be directed towards buds lower down the branch or section of the branch.
April	If weather conditions are right, remove half the bud by pinching with your finger and thumb (*see* Fig 71).
May	New growth should start to form from the pinched bud. This is allowed to develop into healthy growth before being totally removed.
June	Provided that the tree remains healthy and is responding to the training, cut the shoot back to growing point (A), holding the pinched bud. The sap flow which was feeding the terminal bud will now activate several of the dormant buds around point A.
July	If all the buds were allowed to grow, the area would become too clustered, therefore only 2–3 buds should remain. The rest should be removed by rubbing out with your thumb.
Aug–Nov	The remaining buds will produce new growth and this is allowed to continue until December.
December	The older needles are removed to form a smaller needle pad and force new growth. At this time of year, the growth of the tree will slow down and no further training is carried out until the cycle starts again in March.

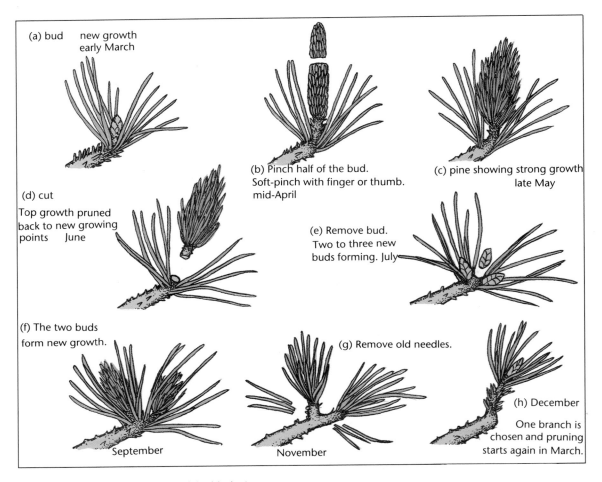

(a) bud   new growth early March

(b) Pinch half of the bud. Soft-pinch with finger or thumb. mid-April

(c) pine showing strong growth late May

(d) cut

Top growth pruned back to new growing points   June

(e) Remove bud. Two to three new buds forming. July

(f) The two buds form new growth.

September

(g) Remove old needles.

November

(h) December

One branch is chosen and pruning starts again in March.

Figs 70 (a)–(h)   The pruning year of the black pine.

Pruning of the Japanese Red Pine

Pinch the young candles during the months of April and May, reducing clusters to two candles, both outward-facing to left and right. In October remove buds – leaving two to restart the cycle in the spring. Removal of needles, as shown with the black pine, is not practised on the red pine.

JUNIPERS

The juniper, like the pine, makes an excellent bonsai tree. The pruning is not as technical as that for pines and pinching can take place throughout the growing season. The two junipers most favoured by bonsai growers are the Chinese juniper (*Juniperus chinesis* 'sargentii') and the needle juniper (*Juniper rigida*). Both trees are excellent for those who wish to grow in the *Sabamiki* style (peeled bark and withered trunk), but they may be difficult to find in your local garden centre. The following list may provide you with a few alternatives.

The foliage on the juniper should be stopped with a pinch made with your finger and thumb (*see* Fig 71) and not tools such as

A Guide to Junipers

Juniperus chinensis
    J. chinensis 'Aurea'
    J. chinensis 'Kaizuka'
    J. chinensis 'Kaizuka Variegata'
    J. chinensis 'Keteleen'   Slow-growing juniper
    J. chinensis 'Pyramidalis'   Dense, slow-growing juniper
    J. chinensis 'Sargentii'
Juniperus communis (common juniper)
    J. communis 'Compressa'   Slow-growing juniper
    J. communis 'Depressa Aurea'
Juniperus horizontalis (creeping juniper)
    J. horizontalis Douglasii'   Long branches
    J. horizontalis 'Glauca'   Long branches
Juniperus japonica 'Blaauw'
    J. japonica 'Mint Julep'
    J. japonica 'Old Gold'
    J. japonica 'Pfitzerana'
    J. japonica 'Pfitzerana Aurea' (golden
      pfitzer)
    J. japonica 'Pfitzerana Compacta'
    J. japonica 'Plumosa'
    J. japonica 'Sulphur Spray'
Juniperus procumbens '(creeping juniper)
    J. procumbens 'Nana'
Juniperus recurva
Juniperus rigida

Fig 72   A Chinese juniper.

Fig 71   Always use the soft-pinch method on the juniper and *never* use pruning tools.

secateurs: when you cut through the cell system, half the cell may be left which then rots back causing the browning. When you use your finger and thumb you tend to pull the cell away from the joint of the next cell and therefore nothing is left to rot back.

JIN

The *Jin* technique involves peeling the bark on a branch to reveal the wood, which is then shaped by splitting, carving and bleaching. Lime sulphur is used to bleach the wood but you will only find it on sale at bonsai nurseries. I personally prefer to use a clear sealant containing a fungicide. The

wood will never become white (it will have a brown tint), but it will still take on an aged appearance. If you do use lime sulphur, make sure to follow all the instructions, such as keeping away from children and pets and using only in well-ventilated areas. You should also cover the soil to prevent the sulphur from damaging the soil particles.

CREATING A DRIFTWOOD PLANTING

The aim is to force the tree to grow and form callouses around a piece or pieces of driftwood. This practice requires both artistic flair and some basic horticultural knowledge of the growing seasons, as well as a good understanding of the tree being used. I prefer to start creating such a bonsai during the months of March and early April, when the tree's sap is slow, but is soon to rise, helping to form callouses very quickly.

Preparation
Step One
First, find a suitable piece of driftwood, such as may be found on a beach. Peel the bark from the wood and allow to dry slowly. You may find that the woody sections will turn brown, if so, this can be easily removed at a later stage. Once the wood has totally dried out, which may take from two months up to a year, the complete piece of wood should be cleaned and made smooth with sandpaper or a sanding machine.

Step Two
You now have to form or enhance the shape of the wood by carving. This is where artistic ability comes into play, but the most important thing is to define the top section and the base of the driftwood. The top section can be any shape of your choosing, but the base will need to be square (*see* Fig 75).

Fig 73 *Sabamiki* and *Jin* are two advanced techniques used to create an 'artistic' bonsai.

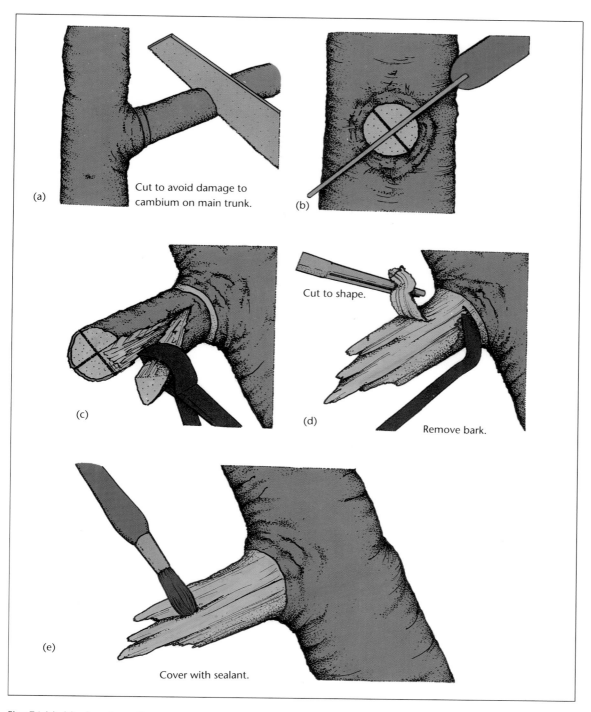

(a) Cut to avoid damage to cambium on main trunk.

(b)

(c)

(d) Cut to shape.

Remove bark.

(e) Cover with sealant.

Figs 74 (a)–(e)   Forming a *Jin*.

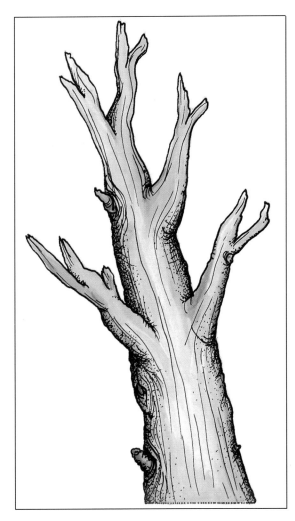

Fig 75   A piece of driftwood, showing the top section and the base.

Step Three

Once you have finished shaping the wood, treat the driftwood to avoid rot. You may use a wood preservative such as that used for treating fences, etc., but you may find that in warm weather, the preservative will give off toxic fumes which will damage the tree's cells and its root system. Therefore, I would suggest using a clear liquid sealant that contains a fungicide, available from your local garden centre. A constant check should be made at all times for rots or diseases such as coral spot, which can live on dead or living wood.

Step Four

After treating the wood, the next stage is to find a suitable tree. Although a few people have tried using deciduous trees with driftwood, I have had more success with the coniferous type of tree, such as the needle juniper. If you cannot find the latter, try another variety from the suggested list of junipers. Cedar is another tree with which I have had success, as is yew, because of its ability to grow from old wood.

Once you have decided on the type of tree you wish to use, you will have to find one whose trunk size is as thick as, if not thicker than, the driftwood. When this is done, take time to study the shape of the tree next to the driftwood, placing them into several different combinations until the correct one is found.

Driftwood Planting

If you are trying out this style for the first time, I would suggest that you look for a tree that already shares some features with the driftwood; i.e., look for a tree that features dead, old and withered wood. Make drawings or take photographs of the complete tree, as well as close-ups of the dead branches and the way in which the living tissues are forming callouses over the dead parts. With the aid of these drawings or photographs, you will be able to copy the design and create something similar with your own bonsai.

Step Five

When all the material has been collected and you have decided on the shape and design of the tree, find a sheltered, frost-free position, away from strong winds and heavy

Fig 76 Driftwood suitable for planting, or wrap-around style, to create an old-looking, gnarled, artistically-formed bonsai.

- Different grades of training wire
- Clips or ties
- Hand mist-sprayer to keep root system moist
- Clamps to hold tree and driftwood securely
- Clear sealant to cover section between driftwood and the tree's tissue.

Method

Step One
Remove the tree from its container and check the roots for pests and diseases. If either are found, do not proceed until the problem is cleared, but remember that the best time for repotting and severe pruning and cutting is during the months of March and early April.

Note Spray roots to stop them from drying out.

Step Two
Place the driftwood next to the trunk or in the position you have chosen, making sure the driftwood is the right way up (flat or square section at the bottom).

Note Spray roots to stop them from drying out.

Step Three
The driftwood has to be placed as tightly as possible against the trunk. Remember that one-third to half the length of the trunk will be removed. Some of the root system may therefore have to be pruned in such a way that it allows space for the flat section of the driftwood.

Note Spray roots to stop them from drying out.

Step Four
With a marking pen, mark the trunk area to be removed. Then, with a sharp, heavy pruning knife, remove that section. Clean the bare woody section with a knife and

rain. This is because the root system can be exposed for up to an hour, so that weather conditions such as frost and strong winds will dry out the root system, giving the tree less chance of survival. It would also be beneficial to have all the items you will need close at hand as shown in the list below.

Suggested item list
- Large and small fork cutters
- Large and small root pruning shears
- Long-handled pruners
- Large and small saw
- Knives, heavy pruning knife and small pen-knife

branches pushed through driftwood

Fig 77 Driftwood can make an elegant addition to your bonsai and enhance the artistic effect of the whole planting.

finally rub down with sandpaper. This will allow the driftwood to fit tightly into the cut, close to the tree. Then, again with your knife, peel the edge of the cut to expose the cambium layer which will help the callous to form around and grip the driftwood.

Note Spray roots to stop them from drying out.

Step Five
Position the driftwood, pushing it in as close as possible to the bare wood of the tree. (The tighter the fit, the more chance of survival for the tree.) Then, place three clamps to hold tree and driftwood together. Place one at the top, one in the centre and one at the bottom.

When you have secured the tree and driftwood in position, use a minimum of six ties from the top of the trunk to the bottom and then paint on the sealant, covering those sections where the live tissue meets the driftwood.

Note Spray roots to stop them from drying out.

[102]

Step Six

Repot the tree in fresh soil into a training pot and place in a sheltered position, away from snow, frost, wind and heavy rain, or shade the tree from direct sunlight and mist the foliage to avoid moisture-loss.

Aftercare

During the next four to six weeks, feed with a foliar feed only. This will allow the root system to recover and form new root hairs. After four to six weeks, normal feeding can take place. Initial placement is very important and a shady position is best.

GROUP PLANTINGS

The main aim of the group is to create an illusion of depth, natural grouping, and an overall 'natural' look, such as may be found in nature, when grown under normal conditions. Depth is created by placing the tallest tree to the front of the group and the smallest tree at the back; natural grouping can be achieved by placing small groups of trees together, or by a single tree with a double trunk. The 'natural' look has to take into account the style of the group; for example, a windswept style reflects the effect of weather conditions found on cliff tops or coastal front where you would find the tree's growth being drawn in one direction. Therefore, attempt to copy that specific style.

Natural Grouping
When a small group of even-numbered trees (say, two trees, for intance) is placed close to another group of odd-numbered trees (three, for instance), the two groups combine to form an overall group of five trees, which makes the complete group an odd-numbered one.

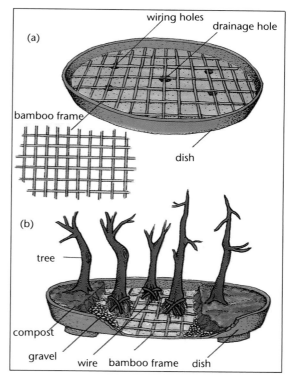

Figs 78 (a) and (b)   A bamboo framework tied to the pot can be used to anchor individual trees in any position in the dish. Tying the trees to the cane grid will also help to stabilize the trees until they become established.

Trunks

All the trunks of your group should be clearly visible and not hidden one behind the other.

Top Growth

The top growth or foliage of the group should follow the general shape of the group, i.e., if the group has its tallest tree at the front and in the centre, the highest point of the foliage will also be at the front and in the centre of the group and then fall away towards the side (*see* Fig 79). The foliage can either form a complete canopy or fall away in pads.

[103]

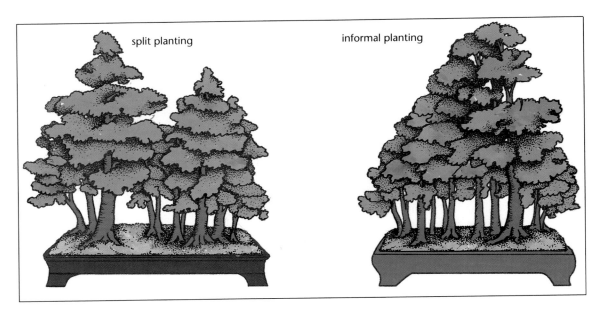

Fig 79   Two styles of group plantings. Split planting is ideal for landscape, and informal planting gives the impression of over grown woodland.

Group plantings can be broken down into four basic categories:

1. 'True' group: made up of individual trees.
2. Raft planting: a group formed from a trunk planted on its side.
3. Landscape: using rocks, etc.
4. Multiple trunk: trees stemming from one root system.

Note It is advisable to start growing bonsai as a single tree. Once the techniques are mastered, and you have made an intense study of the individual tree shapes, you can report your knowledge on group plantings and create completed groups in a chosen style, such as formal upright (*Chokkan*), bending trunks (*Shakan*), etc.

True Group

By 'true', I mean that the trees are all individual specimens. One advantage over groups formed from the same root system is that if one of the trees should die, it can be removed and another tree planted in its place.

The true group always has an odd number of trees: three, five, seven, nine or more, but always in odd numbers.

True Group Planting Styles	
Sambon-yose	Three trunks
Gohon-yose	Five trunks
Nanahon-yose	Seven trunks
Kyuhon-yose	Nine trunks
Yose-ue	More than nine trunks

Although the true group is made up of individual trees, each with their own root system, root pruning, in time, will be a case of removing the complete group from its pot and root pruning the mass root ball, rather than the individual trees.

Step One

(We will take as an example a group with an odd number of trees – the tallest one being at the front of the group). All trees are chosen and trained as individual bonsai trees before being planted as a group, but you should try to keep the individual pots together, so as to see a pattern emerge, with the tallest tree at the front of the group and smaller trees falling away towards the side and the back of the group and prune the trees accordingly. In this way, you will already have a good idea of how the group should look once the individual trees are planted together.

Step Two

Once you are satisfied that the trees are ready and it is the correct time of year for re-potting (March–April), place the trees together to gain some indication of the size of the pot you will need.

Step Three

Before preparing the mesh, gravel and compost, take a look at Fig 78. Here you will see a framework made up of thin bamboo canes (thick training wire can also be used). This frame is used to tie the individual trees into the very shallow dish used for the group planting. By using such a frame, you are not restricted to only placing the trees close to drainage holes, which would otherwise be the only way to wire the groups into position.

Step Four

Once you have made your frame (of either bamboo canes or training wire), place it at the bottom of the pot and secure it with wire that is pushed through the drainage holes and the mesh. Having done this, secure pieces of wire to the frame at the position where you will place your trees. Then continue to fill the bottom of the dish with 6mm gravel, as you would for repotting.

Step Five

Once you have secured the mesh and covered it with gravel, lightly cover the gravel with compost, as for normal repotting. Place the trees in the position you have chosen and tie in each tree with the wire that has been secured to the frame. Cover the root systems with compost down into the root area with a chopstick or dibber. Remember the importance of mixing the compost into the root system.

The aftercare, pruning and wiring is basically the same as for an individual tree, except that the shape of the tree should blend with the rest of the group.

Raft

Raft planting can be broken down into two:

1. Straight-trunk style (*Ikadabuki*). The trunk is laid down on its side; the branches only allowed to develop on one side – growing as individual trees if creating a group effect of a multiple trunk with a long woody base – and undercuts made, which (given the right conditions) will form root.
2. Sinuous style (*Netsunagari*), where several trunks are connected to a single twisted root or roots and connected together either naturally or by grafting, giving the illusion of a fallen tree that is still growing.

Layering can also be used to produce a raft. Choose a stem that has been layered and allowed to develop a continuous root system and anchor it into a training seed tray with 6mm gravel placed at the bottom, in turn covered by a Code 2 compost.

Multiple Trunk

This can be broken down into two:

1. Double trunk (*So-kan*). This is a tree with

Fig 80   A raft (*Ikadabuki*). The trunk leans on its side and the branches are only allowed to develop on one side. The trunk is finally buried, and each branch then treated as an individual trunk, giving the illusion of several trees growing in a clump.

a single root system, but which divides into two trunks near the base of the tree.
2.   Group trunk (*Kabudachi*). This is a single tree at the base which splits into several trunks.

Odd numbers will give the best results. Each trunk is treated as an individual, but at the same time the top growth should blend together as one unit.

Landscapes

Bonsai landscapes can take on many shapes and forms. Groups or single trees can be used and the display may contain rocks, water, bridges and houses. Traditional Japanese landscapes, however, can be groups of

grass, bamboo, bulbs and even bedding plants.

Rock Plantings

Rock plantings are an excellent way of displaying a tree or trees on a rock – either pinned to the top of the rock (*Ishitsuke, see* Fig 81) or planted inside the rock (*Ishitsuki*).

Never use such items as house bricks or pieces of concrete for rocks. Thermal blocks are favoured by many growers because they are easy to carve into shape and because they are porous. Alternatively, visit the countryside, go on cliff walks or obtain permission to visit a local quarry. Try to pick a rock that presents interesting features, with a flat base if possible, as this will help to

[106]

stabilize it when in the dish. If two rocks are used, try to match them up so that the over-all effect is of one piece of rock and not two. Drill holes in the bottom of the rock if it is top-heavy. Wire can be pushed through these holes to anchor the rock to the dish.

When the tree is pinned to the rock, the two most important factors are feeding and watering because of the small amounts of water used and the rapid drainage. Trees growing on rock should be sheltered from strong winds.

Styles used for tree on rock are: cascade (*Kengai*), semi-cascade (*Han-kengai*), wind-swept (*Fukinagashi*), curving or crooked (*Moyogi*), twisted trunk (*Bankan*) and bend-ing trunk (*Shakan*).

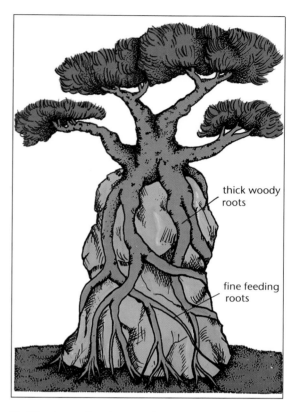

Fig 81   A tree placed over rock.

A List of Trees Suitable for Growing on Rock

Acer buergeriannum (*Kaede*)	Trident maple
Cedrus deoda (*Himaraya-sugi*)	Cedar
Chaenomeles lageneria (*Boke*)	Flowering quince
Crataegus cuneata (*Sanzashi*)	Hawthorn
Forsythia suspensa (*Rengyo*)	Weeping forsythia
Gardenia jasminoides (*Kuchinashi*)	Cape gardenia
Hamamelis japonica (*Mansaku*)	Witch hazel
Picea jezoensis (*Ezo-matsu*)	Ezo spruce
Pinus parviflora (*Goyo-matsu*)	Japanese white pine
Punica granatum (*Zakuro*)	Pomegranate
Rhododendron indicum (*Satsuki*)	Satsuki azalea
Taxus cuspidata (*Ichii*)	Japanese yew
Tsuga diversifolia (*Kometsugu*)	Japanese hemlock
Wisteria floribunda (*Fuji*)	Japanese wisteria

Root Over Rock

In the root-over-rock style, the tree's roots are exposed. There are two methods:

1.   Find a tree which has two, three or more thick, woody roots extending from the base of the trunk. The tree can then saddle the rock, and its roots can be pinned to the side of the rock. The tree is then buried up to a few centimetres past the base of the trunk in the soil or repotted into a large container and left to recover for the first year.

In the second year, one-third of the soil is removed and all fibrous roots found on the exposed woody roots should be re-moved; as the roots are exposed to the air they will thicken and age. In the third year, another third is exposed and again all fibrous

Figs 82 (a) and (b)   Trident maple grown over rock. The roots form intricate patterns and can thus add to the beauty of the tree.

A List of Trees Suitable for Growing over Rock

Acer buergeriannum (*Kaede*)	Trident maple	*Picea jazoensis* (*Ezo-matsu*)	Ezo spruce
Cedrus deoda (*Himaraya-sugi*)	Cedar	*Pinus parviflora* (*Goyo-matsu*)	Japanese white pine
Chaenomeles lageneria (*Boke*)	Flowering quince	*Punica granatum* (*Zakuro*)	Pomegranate
Crataegus cuneata (*Sanzashi*)	Hawthorn	*Rhododendron indicum* (*Satsuki*)	Satsuki azalea
Forsythia suspensa (*Rengyo*)	Weeping forsythia	*Taxus cuspidata* (*Ichii*)	Japanese yew
Gardenia jasminoides (*Kuchinashi*)	Cape gardenia	*Tsuga diversifolia* (*Kometsuga*)	Japanese hemlock
Hamamelis japonica (*Mansaku*)	Witch hazel	*Wisteria floribunda* (*Fuji*)	Japanese wisteria

roots are removed, leaving clean, woody roots. At the beginning of the fourth year, and provided that the roots are showing signs of gripping the rock, the complete tree, rock and root system can be removed from the soil or container and root-pruned in the normal way.

2. Graft on a root system, as shown earlier in this chapter.

Suitable for the root-over-rock style are cascade (*Kengai*), semi-cascade (*Han-kengai*), windswept (*Fukinagashi*), curving (*Moyogi*), twisted trunk (*Bankan*) and bending trunk (*Shakan*).

Part II

Chapter 8

AN A–Z OF HARDY BONSAI

In this chapter, I have tried to list as many hardy trees and shrubs as possible for hardy (outdoor) bonsai, but the choice eventually rests with you.

ACER (Maple)

There are several varieties of maple, most of them originating from Japan. The Japanese maple, *Acer palmatum*, is a small, shrub-like tree which is very slow-growing and produces a pleasant autumn colour. Other *palmatum* forms, such as the *Acer*

Japanese red maple (*Acer rubra*) showing spring colours. Note the twin trunk.

Styles for the Maples

Chokkan   Formal upright or straight-trunk style.
Moyogi   Curving or informal upright trunk.
Shakan   Leaning or slanting trunk.
Bankan   Twisted trunk, coiled almost like a spring.
So-kan   Double trunk which divides close to the base of the trunk.
San-kan   Triple trunk.
Go-kan   Five trunks.
Kabudachi   Multiple trunk – single tree at the base, splitting into several trunks to form a group.
Han-kengai   Semi-cascade.
Kengai   Cascade.
Neagari   Exposed root system.
Ishitsuki   Tree or trees grown on a rock.

palmatum 'Senkaki' (coral bark maple), with its coral-red branches gives excellent winter colour. *Acer palmatum* 'Dissectum' has a leaf which is divided into five to nine pinnatifid lobes, as opposed to *Acer palmatum* which has a solid leaf structure. *Acer griseum* (paperbark maple), which originated from China, has a bark which flakes to expose a coloured underbark. *Acer campestre* (field maple) came from west Asia, but has been growing in Britain for many years. The autumn colour of that tree can be a bright yellow, or sometimes yellow with a red tinge. *Acer pseudoplatanus* (sycamore) also originated from west Asia, but has long been grown in Britain. The leaves on the sycamore tend to be on the large side, so that it will need root and leaf pruning every year.

[110]

Acer campestre (field maple)

Habit   Deciduous. Medium-sized tree, formal style.
Compost   Code 5. (The field maple likes heavy compost). Do not let the compost become too dry.
Position   Moist conditions.
Root pruning   Every year for up to five years, then every two to three.

Japanese maple (*Acer palmatum*).

Wiring   Wire during the growing season. Cover wire to protect bark, remove after six months.
Propagation   Seed, cutting or grafting.
Pests   Aphids: spray with soapy water.
Diseases   Canker, coral spot, die-back, tar spot and powdery mildew.

Acer griseum (paperbark maple)

Habit   Deciduous. Slow-growing, trunk flakes to show underbark, suits most styles.

Compost   Code 3. Open, well-drained, sandy compost.
Position   Part-shade or sun. Dislikes strong winds.
Root pruning   Every year for up to five years, then every two.
Wiring   During the growing season. Cover wire to protect bark, remove after six months.
Propagation   Seed, cutting or grafting.
Pests   Aphids: spray with soapy water.
Diseases   Canker, coral spot, die-back, tar spot and powdery mildew.

Acer grosseri (snake-bark maple)

Habit   Deciduous. Slow-growing, very attractive bark, suits most styles.
Compost   Code 3. Open, well-drained, sandy compost.
Position   Part-shade or sun. Dislikes strong winds.
Root pruning   Every year for up to five years, then every two.
Wiring   During the growing season. Cover wire to protect bark, remove after six months.
Propagation   Seed, cutting or grafting.
Pests   Aphids: spray with soapy water.
Diseases   Canker, coral spot, die-back, tar spot and powdery mildew.

Acer japonicum 'Aureum'

Habit   Deciduous. Slow-growing, yellow leaves.
Compost   Code 3. Open, well-drained, sandy compost.
Position   Part-shade. Sun will scorch the leaves.
Root pruning   Every year for up to five years, then every two.
Wiring   During the growing season. Cover wire to protect bark, remove after six months.
Propagation   Seed, cutting or grafting.
Pests   Aphids: spray with soapy water.
Diseases   Canker, coral spot, die-back, tar spot and powdery mildew.

Acer palmatum (all types)

Habit   Deciduous. Slow-growing with good autumn colour, suits most styles.

Acer palmatum (rubra). The red leaf reverts to green if it is not leaf-pruned.

Compost   Code 3. Open, well-drained, sandy compost.
Position   Part-shade. Dislikes strong winds and frost.
Root pruning   Every year for up to five years, then every two or three.
Wiring   During the growing season. Cover wire to protect bark, remove after six months.
Propagation   Seed, cutting or grafting.
Pests   Aphids: spray with soapy water.
Diseases   Canker, coral spot, die-back, tar spot and powdery mildew.

Acer pseudoplatanus (sycamore)

Habit   Deciduous. Large, fairly fast-growing tree, formal or informal style.
Compost   Code 4, but will tolerate most composts.

Position   Will tolerate part-shade or sun.
Root pruning   Every year for the first fifteen years, then every two to three.
Wiring   During the growing season. Remove after six months.
Propagation   Seed, cutting or grafting.
Pests   Aphids: spray with insecticide or soapy water.
Diseases   Canker, coral spot, die-back, tar spot and powdery mildew.

Acer plantanoides 'Crimson King' (Norway maple)

Habit   Deciduous. Fast-growing, hardy, leaves purple-red.
Compost   Code 4, but will tolerate most composts.
Position   Part-shade or full sun.

Colourful variegated maple will not tolerate complete pruning.

[112]

Mountain maple (old specimen), showing autumn colours.

Root pruning Every year for up to ten years, then every two.
Wiring During the growing season. Remove after six months.
Propagation Seed, cutting or grafting.
Pests Aphids: spray with soapy water.
Diseases Canker, coral spot, die-back, tar spot and powdery mildew.

Acacia

See Chapter 9.

AESCULUS (Horse Chestnut)

The horse chestnut is one of the most widely known trees in Britain. Popular with young children for its seed (conkers) which, if planted, will germinate quite easily. (It is thus ideal for the beginner).

Aesculus hippocastanum is the common horse chestnut and bears white flowers in May, but it will take a number of years before it will flower as a bonsai. There are two other forms of the horse chestnut, *Aesculus hippocastanum* 'Pumila', a dwarf form with smaller leaves, and *Aesculus indica* (Indian horse chestnut) that produces pink-flushed flowers. The leaves on the common and the Indian varieties will need leaf pruning every year to keep them in proportion with the rest of the tree.

Aesculus (horse chestnut). This tree measures 42cm (16in) and is aged fifteen, grown from seed.

Aesculus arguta

Habit Deciduous small tree with soft creamy-white flowers.
Compost Code 5. Heavy, moist compost with free drainage.
Position Part-shade or sun.
Root pruning Every year for up to fifteen years, then every two.
Wiring During the growing season. Remove wire after six months.

[113]

Propagation Seeds sown in pots or in a prepared site in the garden, or grafting.
Pests Mainly trouble-free.
Diseases Coral spot, die-back.

Aesculus californica

Habit Deciduous. Bears fragrant white (sometimes pink) flowers.
Compost Code 5. Heavy, moist compost with free drainage.
Position Part-shade or sun.
Root pruning Every year for up to fifteen years, then every two.
Wiring During the growing season. Remove wire after six months.
Propagation Seeds sown in pots or in a prepared site in the garden, or grafting.
Pests Mainly trouble-free.
Diseases Coral spot, die-back.

Styles for the Horse Chestnut

Chokkan Formal upright or straight-trunk style.
Moyogi Curving or informal upright trunk.
Shakan Leaning or slanting trunk.
So-kan Double trunk which divides close to the base of the trunk.
Neagari Exposed root system.

Aesculus x carnea

Habit Deciduous, (pink flowers increasingly popular).
Compost Code 5. Heavy moist compost with free drainage.
Position Part-shade or sun.
Root pruning Every year for up to fifteen years, then every two.
Wiring During the growing season. Remove wire after six months.
Propagation Seeds sown in pots or in a prepared site in the garden, or grafting.
Pests Mainly trouble-free.
Diseases Coral spot, die-back.

Aesculus chinensis

Habit Deciduous. Rare, slow-growing tree originating from China, bears white flowers.
Compost Code 5. Heavy, moist compost with free drainage.
Position Part-shade or sun.
Root pruning Every year for up to fifteen years, then every two.
Wiring During the growing season. Remove wire after six months.
Propagation Seeds sown in pots or in a prepared site in the garden; alternatively, grafting.
Pests Mainly trouble-free.
Diseases Coral spot, die-back.

Aesculus hippocastanum

Habit Deciduous and hardy. Common horse chestnut: frequently seen and easily recognized variety throughout Britain. Bears white flowers.
Compost Code 5. Heavy moist compost with free drainage.
Position Part-shade or sun.
Root pruning Every year for up to fifteen years, then every two.
Wiring During the growing season. Remove wire after six months.
Propagation Seeds sown in pots or in a prepared site in the garden, or grafting.
Pests Mainly trouble-free.
Diseases Coral spot, die-back.

Aesculus hippocastanum 'Pumila'

Habit Deciduous. Dwarf variety.
Compost Code 5. Heavy moist compost with free drainage.
Position Part-shade or sun.
Root pruning Every year for up to fifteen years, then every two.
Wiring During the growing season. Remove wire after six months.
Propagation Seeds sown in pots or in a prepared site in the garden, or grafting.
Pests Mainly trouble-free.
Diseases Coral spot, die-back.

Aesculus x mississippiensis

Habit Deciduous. Small tree with deep-red flowers with distinct yellow stamens.
Compost Code 5. Heavy moist compost with free drainage.
Position Part-shade or sun.
Root pruning Every year for up to fifteen years, then every two.
Wiring During the growing season. Remove wire after six months.
Propagation Seeds sown in pots or in a prepared site in the garden; alternativley, grafting.
Pests Mainly trouble-free.
Diseases Coral spot, die-back.

Aesculus x mutabilis

Habit Deciduous. Small tree with yellow and red flowers.
Compost Code 5. Heavy moist compost with free drainage.
Position Part-shade or sun.
Root pruning Every year for up to fifteen years, then every two.
Wiring During the growing season. Remove wire after six months.
Propagation Seeds sown in pots or in a prepared site in the garden; alternativley, grafting.
Pests Mainly trouble-free.
Diseases Coral spot, die-back.

Aesculus pavia

Habit Deciduous. Small tree with crimson flowers.
Compost Code 5. Heavy moist compost with free drainage.
Position Part-shade or sun.
Root pruning Every year for up to fifteen years, then every two.
Wiring During the growing season. Remove wire after six months.
Propagation Seeds sown in pots or in a prepared site in the garden; alternativley, grafting.
Pests Mainly trouble-free.
Diseases Coral spot, die-back.

Aesculus splendens

Habit Deciduous. Bears attractive scarlet flowers.
Compost Code 5. Heavy, moist compost with free drainage.
Position Part-shade or sun.
Root pruning Every year for up to fifteen years, then every two.
Wiring During the growing season. Remove wire after six months.
Propagation Seeds sown in pots or in a prepared site in the garden, or grafting.
Pests Mainly trouble-free.
Diseases Coral spot, die-back.

Aesculus turbinata

Habit Deciduous, very large foliage, veined. Flowers are white/yellow with red spot.
Compost Code 5. Heavy, moist compost with free drainage.
Position Part-shade or sun.
Root pruning Every year for up to fifteen years, then every two.
Wiring During the growing season. Remove wire after six months.
Propagation Seeds sown in pots or in a prepared site in the garden, or grafting.
Pests Mainly trouble-free.
Diseases Coral spot, die-back.

ALNUS (Alder)

The alder can be found in Europe, Siberia and the northern regions of Africa.

Alnus firma

Habit Deciduous. Small tree with well-defined leaves.
Compost Code 3.
Position Moisture, sun or part-shade.
Root pruning March–April.
Wiring March.
Propagation Seed, cuttings.
Pests Aphids.
Diseases Mainly trouble-free.

Styles for the Alder

Chokkan   Formal upright or straight-trunk style.
Moyogi   Curving or informal upright trunk.
Shakan   Leaning or slanting trunk.
Bankan   Twisted trunk, coiled almost like a spring.
So-kan   Double trunk which divides close to the base of the trunk.
San-kan   Triple trunk.
Go-kan   Five trunks.
Kabudachi   Multiple trunk – single tree at the base, splitting into several trunks to form a group.
Han-kengai   Semi-cascade.
Kengai   Cascade.
Neagari   Exposed root system.
Ishitsuki   Tree or trees grown on a rock.

Alnus glutinosa

Habit   Deciduous. One of the most commonly seen alders in Britain. Small tree producing catkins in spring.
Compost   Code 3.
Position   Moisture, sun or part-shade.
Root pruning   March–April.
Wiring   March.
Propagation   Seed or cuttings.
Pests   Aphids, caterpillars.
Diseases   Mainly trouble-free.

Alnus glutinosa 'Aurea'

Habit   Deciduous. Pale yellow leaves.
Compost   Code 3.
Position   Moisture, sun or part-shade.
Root pruning   March–April.
Wiring   March.
Propagation   Seed or cuttings.
Pests   Aphids, caterpillars.
Diseases   Mainly trouble-free.

Alnus glutinosa incisa

Habit   Deciduous. Small leaves.
Compost   Code 3.
Position   Moisture, sun or part-shade.

Root pruning   March–April.
Wiring   March.
Propagation   Seed or cuttings.
Pests   Aphids, caterpillars.
Diseases   Mainly trouble-free.

Alnus glutinosa 'Pyramidalis'

Habit   Deciduous. As name suggests, branches form into a pyramid shape.
Compost   Code 3.
Position   Moisture, sun or part-shade.
Root pruning   March–April.
Wiring   March.
Propagation   Seed or cuttings.
Pests   Aphids, caterpillars.
Diseases   Mainly trouble-free.

AMELANCHIER (Snowy Mespilus or June Berry)

Known for both its flowers and fruits as well as its bright autumn colour.

Amelanchier alnifolia

Habit   Deciduous, hardy small tree. Flowers in spring, followed by black fruit.
Compost   Code 3.
Position   Lime-free soil.

Styles for the Amelanchier

Chokkan   Formal upright or straight-trunk style.
Moyogi   Curving or informal upright trunk.
Shakan   Leaning or slanting trunk.
Bankan   Twisted trunk, coiled almost like a spring.
So-kan   Double trunk which divides close to the base of the trunk.
Kabudachi   Multiple trunk – single tree at the base, splitting into several trunks to form a group.
Bankan   Twisted trunk, coiled almost like a spring.
Neagari   Exposed root system.

Root pruning March–April.
Wiring March.
Propagation Seed or cuttings.
Pests Aphids, caterpillars.
Diseases Mainly trouble-free.

Amelanchier canadensis

Habit Deciduous, hardy small tree.
Compost Code 3.
Position Moist conditions, sun or shade.
Root pruning March–April.
Wiring March.
Propagation Seed or cuttings.
Pests Aphids.
Diseases Mainly trouble-free.

Amelanchier florida

Habit Deciduous, hardy small tree. Produces purple fruit and attractive yellow leaves in the autumn.
Compost Code 3.
Position Sun or shade.
Root pruning March–April.
Wiring March.
Propagation Seed or cuttings.
Pests Aphids.
Diseases Mainly trouble-free.

Amelanchier laevis

Habit Deciduous, hardy small tree. Pink foliage and fragrant white flowers in May followed by attractive autumn shades.
Compost Code 3.
Position Sun or shade.
Root pruning March–April.
Wiring March.
Propagation Seed or cuttings.
Pests Aphids.
Diseases Mainly trouble-free.

ARBUTUS (Strawberry Tree)

This small, evergreen tree can make an excellent bonsai and with age the trunk and branches of *Arbutus andrachnoides* will transform into a cinnamon-red colour. The tree produces white

---

Styles for the Strawberry Tree

Chokkan Formal upright or straight-trunk style.
Moyogi Curving or informal upright trunk.
Shakan Leaning or slanting trunk.
Bankan Twisted trunk, coiled almost like a spring.
So-kan Double trunk which divides close to the base of the trunk.
Neagari Exposed root system.

---

flowers during the late autumn and early winter, followed by strawberry-like fruits, which are inedible. The glossy green leaves are inclined to be too large for a bonsai tree, so that you will need to leaf-prune over a period of several years before creating a smaller leaf.

Arbutus andrachnoides

Habit Deciduous. Small, slow growing-tree, with strawberry-like fruits and a colourful bark.
Compost Code 4 or 3.
Position Sun or part-shade.
Root pruning Every year for up to ten years, then every two.
Wiring During the growing season. Cover wire to protect bark, remove after six months.
Propagation Seeds or cuttings.
Pests Mainly trouble-free.
Diseases Coral spot, die-back.

ARUNDINARIA (Bamboo)

Arundinaria japonica

Most common form.

Arundinaria nitida

Forms a dense clump.

Arundinaria pygmaea

Habit Carpet-forming bamboo, ideal for bonsai.

Compost Code 4.
Position Part-shade or sun.
Root pruning Every year for up to five years, then every two.
Wiring During the growing season. Cover wire to protect bark, remove after six months.
Pests Mainly trouble-free.
Diseases Mildew.

Styles for the Bamboo

Go-kan Five trunks.
Kabudachi Multiple trunk – single tree at the base, splitting into several trunks to form a group.
Ishitsuki Tree or trees planted on a rock.

AZALEA

See Rhododendron.

BETULA (Silver Birch)

Many people recognize the *Betula* by the silver bark which gives it its name. *Betula pendula*, which produces the silver bark, makes a good substitute for the Japanese white beech, chosen by the Japanese for group plantings.

Betula albo-sinensis

Habit Originated in China. Red and pink bark.
Compost Code 4 or 5, but not too wet.
Position Sun or part-shade.
Root pruning Every year for up to five years, then every two.
Wiring March–April. Remove totally after six months.
Propagation Seeds or grafting.
Pests Caterpillars.
Diseases Canker, coral spot, die-back.

Styles for the Silver Birch

Chokkan Formal upright or straight-trunk style.
Moyogi Curving or informal upright trunk.
Shakan Leaning or slanting trunk.
Bankan Twisted trunk, coiled almost like a spring.
So-kan Double trunk which divides close to the base of the trunk.
Kabudachi Multiple-trunk – single tree at the base, splitting into several trunks to form a group.
Hokidachi Broom style – the head or foliage is shaped like a broom.
Fukinagashi Windswept style – all the branches lean in one direction.
Neagari Exposed root system.
Netsuranari Connecting-root style – an odd number of trees growing from the same root system.
Ikadabuki Raft style – the trunk leans on its side and the branches are only allowed to develop on one side, giving the impression of several trees growing in a clump.
Yose-ue Group planting which resembles a forest.

Betula chinensis

Habit Small tree from China. Small leaves.
Compost Code 4 or 5, but not too wet.
Position Sun or part-shade.
Root pruning Every year for up to five years, then every two.
Wiring March–April. Remove after six months.
Propagation Seeds or grafting.
Pests Caterpillars.
Diseases Canker, coral spot, die-back.

Betula davurica

Habit Prefers colder climates. Unusual bark.
Compost Code 4 or 5, but not too wet.
Position Sun or part-shade.
Root pruning Every year for up to five years, then every two.
Wiring March–April. Remove wire after six months.

Propagation   Seeds or grafting.
Pests   Caterpillars.
Diseases   Canker, coral spot, die-back.

Betula nana (dwarf birch)

Habit   Small tree and small foliage.
Compost   Code 4 or 5, but not too wet.
Position   Sun or part-shade.
Root pruning   Every year for up to five years, then every two.
Wiring   March–April. Remove after six months.
Propagation   Seeds or grafting.
Pests   Caterpillars.
Diseases   Canker, coral spot, die-back.

Betula nigra (river birch)

Habit   Enjoys moist areas.
Compost   Code 4 or 5, keep well dampened.
Position   Sun or shade.
Root pruning   Every year for up to five years, then every two.
Wiring   March–April. Remove after six months.
Propagation   Seeds or grafting.
Pests   Caterpillars.
Diseases   Canker, coral spot, die-back.

Betula papyrifera (paper birch)

Habit   Tends to be a large tree. Attractive autumnal colouring.
Compost   Code 4 or 5, but not too wet.
Position   Sun or part-shade.
Root pruning   Every year for up to five years, then every two.
Wiring   March–April. Remove after six months.
Propagation   Seeds or grafting.
Pests   Caterpillars.
Diseases   Canker, coral-spot, die-back.

Betula pendula (common silver birch)

Habit   Fast-growing tree.
Compost   Code 4 or 5, but not too wet.
Position   Sun or part-shade.
Root pruning   Every year for up to five years, then every two.

Wiring   During the growing season. Cover wire to protect bark, remove after six months.
Propagation   Seeds or grafting.
Pests   Caterpillars.
Diseases   Canker, coral spot, die-back.

Betula pendula 'Dentata Viscosa'

Habit   Small tree, but not over-attractive.
Compost   Code 4 or 5, but not too wet.
Position   Sun or part-shade.
Root pruning   Every year for up to five years, then every two.
Wiring   March–April. Cover wire during growing season to protect bark, remove after six months.
Propagation   Seeds or grafting.
Pests   Caterpillars.
Diseases   Canker, coral spot, die-back.

Betula pendula 'Purpurea' (purple leaf birch)

Habit   Slow-growing tree, purple leaves.
Compost   Code 4 or 5, but not too wet.
Position   Sun or part-shade.
Root pruning   Every year for up to five years, then every two.
Wiring   March–April. Remove after six months.
Propagation   Seeds or grafting.
Pests   Caterpillars.
Diseases   Canker, coral spot, die-back.

Betula pendula 'Youngii' (Young's weeping birch)

Habit   Small tree, prone to weeping and developing a 'dome' shape.
Compost   Code 4 or 5, but not too wet.
Position   Sun or part-shade.
Root pruning   Every year for up to five years, then every two.
Wiring   March–April. Cover wire during growing season to protect bark, remove after six months.
Propagation   Seeds or grafting.
Pests   Caterpillars.
Diseases   Canker, coral spot, die-back.

Betula pubescens (common white birch)

Habit   Attractive tree with a reddish bark. Enjoys damp situations.
Compost   Code 3.
Position   Sun or part-shade.
Root pruning   Every year for up to five years, then every two.
Wiring   March–April. Cover wire during growing season to protect bark, remove totally after six months.
Propagation   Seeds or grafting.
Pests   Caterpillars.
Diseases   Canker, coral spot, die-back.

BUXUS (Box)

A small, evergreen bush making excellent bonsai material.

Buxus, commonly known as box. This is very slow-growing. An ideal bonsai for the beginner.

Styles for the Box Tree

Chokkan   Formal upright or straight-trunk style.
Moyogi   Curving or informal upright trunk.
Shakan   Leaning or slanting trunk.
Bankan   Twisted trunk, coiled almost like a spring.
So-kan   Double trunk which divides close to the base of the trunk.
Kabudachi   Multiple trunk – single tree at the base, splitting into several trunks to form a group.
Hokidachi   Broom style – the head or foliage is shaped like a broom.
Fukinagashi   Windswept style – all the branches lean in one direction.
Neagari   Exposed root system.
Netsuranari   Connecting-root style – an odd number of trees growing from the same root system.
Ikadabuki   Raft style – the trunk leans on its side and the branches are only allowed to develop on one side, giving the illusion of several trees growing in a clump.
Yose-ue   Group planting which resembles a forest.

Buxus microphylla

Habit   Small tree, originally from Japan.
Compost   Code 3.
Position   Sun or shade.
Root pruning   March–April.
Wiring   March.
Propagation   Seed, cuttings or division.
Pests   Mainly trouble-free.
Diseases   Mainly trouble-free.

Buxus microphylla 'Compacta'

Habit   Naturally small tree, ideal for bonsai.
Compost   Code 3.
Position   Sun or shade.
Root pruning   March–April.
Wiring   March.
Propagation   Seed, cuttings or division.
Pests   Mainly trouble-free.
Diseases   Mainly trouble-free.

Buxus microphylla 'Green Pillow'

Habit   Slow-growing tree.
Compost   Code 3.
Position   Sun or shade.
Root pruning   March–April.
Wiring   March.
Propagation   Seed, cuttings or division.
Pests   Mainly trouble-free.
Diseases   Mainly trouble-free.

Buxus microphylla japonica

Habit   Small tree.
Compost   Code 3.
Position   Sun or shade.
Root pruning   March–April.
Wiring   March.
Propagation   Seed, cuttings or division.
Pests   Mainly trouble-free.
Diseases   Mainly trouble-free.

Buxus microphylla koreana

Habit   Small tree, bright green leaves.
Compost   Code 3.
Position   Sun or shade.
Root pruning   March–April.
Wiring   March.
Propagation   Seed, cuttings or division.
Pests   Mainly trouble-free.
Diseases   Mainly trouble-free.

Buxus sempervirens 'Aurea Pendula'

Habit   Small tree, creamy-yellow mottled leaves.
Compost   Code 3.
Position   Sun or shade.
Root pruning   March–April.
Wiring   March.
Propagation   Seed, cuttings or division.
Pests   Mainly trouble-free.
Diseases   Mainly trouble-free.

Buxus sempervirens 'Aureovariegata'

Habit   Small tree, creamy-yellow mottled leaves.
Compost   Code 3.
Position   Sun or shade.
Root pruning   March–April.
Wiring   March.
Propagation   Seed, cuttings or division.
Pests   Mainly trouble-free.
Diseases   Mainly trouble-free.

Buxus sempervirens 'Prostrata'

Habit   Branches tend to grow horizontally.
Compost   Code 3.
Position   Sun or shade.
Root pruning   March–April.
Wiring   March.
Propagation   Seed, cuttings or division.
Pests   Mainly trouble-free.
Diseases   Mainly trouble-free.

CALLICARPA

Small shrub with colourful fruits and good autumn colour.

Styles for the Callicarpa

Chokkan   Formal upright or straight-trunk style.
Moyogi   Curving or informal upright trunk.
Shakan   Leaning or slanting trunk.
Bankan   Twisted trunk, coiled almost like a spring.
So-kan   Double trunk which divides close to the base of the trunk.
Kabudachi   Multiple trunk – single tree at the base, splitting into several trunks to form a group.
Hokidachi   Broom style – the head or foliage is shaped like a broom.
Fukinagashi   Windswept style – all the branches lean in one direction.
Neagari   Exposed root system.
Yose-ue   Group planting which resembles a forest.

Callicarpa bodinieri

Habit   Small tree. Deep lilac fruit and elongated leaves, attractive autumnal shades.
Compost   Code 3 or 4.
Position   Sun or part-shade.
Root pruning   March.
Wiring   March.
Propagation   Seed or cuttings.
Pests   Mainly trouble-free.
Diseases   Mainly trouble-free.

CARPINUS (Hornbeam)

The hornbeam makes an excellent bonsai and is often used by the Japanese, whether grown as a single bonsai specimen or in a group style. *Carpinus betulus* is the common hornbeam. Its sturdy-looking grey trunk is a very noticeable feature when grown as a large thick-trunk specimen bonsai, either in the formal upright style (*Chok-*

Hornbeam, at the beginning of its bonsai life.

kan), or curved, informal upright style (*Moyogi*). *Carpinus japonica* is a smaller, wide-spreading hornbeam suitable for the broom style (*Hokidachi*). The tree produces catkins and is probably better suited to bonsai than *Carpinus betulus*.

Carpinus betulus (common hornbeam)

Habit   Deciduous.
Compost   Code 4, but will do well in most types of compost.
Position   Sun or part shade.
Root pruning   March–April.
Wiring   During the growing season. Remove wire after six months.
Propagation   Seeds or grafting.
Pests   Caterpillars.
Diseases   Coral spot, die-back, powdery mildew.

Styles for the Hornbeam

Chokkan   Formal upright or straight-trunk style.
Moyogi   Curving or informal upright trunk.
Shakan   Leaning or slanting trunk.
Bankan   Twisted trunk, coiled almost like a spring.
So-kan   Double trunk which divides close to the base of the trunk.
Kabudachi   Multiple trunk – single tree at the base, splitting into several trunks to form a group.
Hokidachi   Broom style – the head or foliage is shaped like a broom.
Fukinagashi   Windswept style – all the branches lean in one direction.
Neagari   Exposed root system.
Netsuranari   Connecting-root style – an odd number of trees growing from the same root system.
Ikadabuki   Raft style – the trunk leans on its side and the branches are only allowed to develop on one side, giving the illusion of several trees growing in a clump.
Yose-ue   Group planting which resembles a forest.

[122]

Carpinus betulus 'Columnaris'

Habit Deciduous, slow-growing.
Compost Code 4, but will do well in most types of compost.
Position Sun or part-shade.
Root pruning Every year for up to five years, then every two.
Wiring During the growing season. Remove wire after six months.
Propagation Seeds or grafting.
Pests Caterpillars.
Diseases Coral spot, die-back, powdery mildew.

Carpinus betulus 'Fastigiata'

Habit Deciduous.
Compost Code 4, but will do well in most types of compost.
Position Sun or part-shade.
Root pruning March–April.
Wiring During the growing season. Remove wire after six months.
Propagation Seeds or grafting.
Pests Caterpillars.
Diseases Coral spot, die-back, powdery mildew.

Carpinus betulus 'Pendula'

Habit Deciduous small tree.
Compost Code 4, but will do well in most types of compost.
Position Sun or part-shade.
Root pruning March–April.
Wiring During the growing season. Remove wire after six months.
Propagation Seeds or grafting.
Pests Caterpillars.
Diseases Coral spot, die-back, powdery mildew.

Carpinus betulus 'Purpurea'

Habit Deciduous. Purple tinge to new leaves; will need leaf pruning in June to retain colour.
Compost Code 4, but will do well in most types of compost.
Position Sun or part-shade.
Root pruning March–April.

Wiring During the growing season. Remove wire after six months.
Propagation Seeds or grafting.
Pests Caterpillars.
Diseases Coral spot, die-back and powdery mildew.

Carpinus japonica

Habit Deciduous, attractive small tree from Japan.
Compost Code 4, but will do well in most types of compost.
Position Sun or part-shade.
Root pruning March–April.
Wiring During the growing season. Remove wire after six months.
Propagation Seeds or grafting.
Pests Caterpillars.
Diseases Coral spot, die-back and powdery mildew.

Carpinus orientalis

Habit Deciduous small tree.
Compost Code 4, but will do well in most types of compost.
Position Sun or part-shade.
Root pruning March–April.
Wiring During the growing season. Remove wire after six months.
Propagation Seeds or grafting.
Pests Caterpillars.
Diseases Coral spot, die-back and powdery mildew.

Carpinus turczaninowii

Habit Deciduous. Bears small leaves, new leaves bright red.
Compost Code 4, but will do well in most types of compost.
Position Sun or part-shade.
Root pruning March–April.
Wiring During the growing season. Remove wire after six months.
Propagation Seeds or grafting.
Pests Caterpillars.
Diseases Coral spot, die-back, and powdery mildew.

CATALPA (Indian Bean Tree)

The catalpa is a tree for the collector. The disadvantage of this tree is the size of its leaves, which (even with leaf pruning) is far too big for the tree. However, the catalpa can make a good specimen tree when grown to a metre in height.

Styles for the Catalpa

Chokkan   Formal upright or straight-trunk style.
Moyogi   Curving or informal upright trunk.
Shakan   Leaning or slanting trunk.
Bankan   Twisted trunk, coiled almost like a spring.
So-kan   Double trunk which divides close to the base of the trunk.
Hokidachi   Broom style – the head or foliage is shaped like a broom.
Fukinagashi   Windswept style – all the branches lean in one direction.
Neagari   Exposed root system.

Catalpa bignonioides

Habit   White flowers with purple and yellow markings. Place in wind-protected area.
Compost   Code 4.
Position   Sun or part-shade.
Root pruning   March–April.
Wiring   March.
Propagation   Seed.
Pests   Aphids, caterpillars.
Diseases   Mainly trouble-free.

Catalpa bignonioides 'Aurea' (golden Indian bean tree)

Habit   Soft-yellow, velvety leaves that tend to be large.
Compost   Code 4.
Position   Sun or shade.
Root pruning   March–April.
Wiring   March.
Propagation   Seed.
Pests   Aphids, caterpillars.
Diseases   Mainly trouble-free.

Catalpa bignonioides 'Nana'

Habit   Small, interesting tree.
Compost   Code 4.
Position   Sun or shade.
Root pruning   March–April.
Wiring   March.
Propagation   Seed.
Pests   Aphids, caterpillars.
Diseases   Mainly trouble-free.

Catalpa bignonioides 'Variegata'

Habit   As name suggests, leaves are variegated or creamy-yellow.
Compost   Code 4.
Position   Sun or shade.
Root pruning   March–April.
Wiring   March.
Propagation   Seed.
Pests   Aphids, caterpillars.
Diseases   Mainly trouble-free.

Catalpa bungei 'Purpurea'

Habit   New leaves dark purple, turning to deep green.
Compost   Code 4.
Position   Sun or shade.
Root pruning   March.
Wiring   March.
Propagation   Seed.
Pests   Aphids, caterpillars.
Diseases   Mainly trouble-free.

CEDRUS (Cedar)

Cedrus libani (cedar of Lebanon)

Spreading tree with horizontal branches.

Cedrus atantica (Atlantic cedar)

Pyramid shape.

Cedrus deodora (deodar)

Habit   Pyramid shape with hanging branches.
Compost   Code 4.
Position   Part-shade or sun.
Root pruning   Every year for up to five years, then every two.
Wiring   During the growing season.
Propagation   Seed or cutting.
Pests   Mainly trouble-free.
Diseases   Mainly trouble-free.

Styles for the Cedar

Chokkan   Formal upright or straight-trunk style.
Moyogi   Curving or informal upright trunk.
Shakan   Leaning or slanting trunk.
Bankan   Twisted trunk, coiled almost like a spring.
So-kan   Double trunk which divides close to the base of the trunk.
San-kan   Triple trunk.
Go-kan   Five trunks.
Kabudachi   Multiple trunk – single tree at the base, splitting into several trunks to form a group.

CELASTRUS (Bittersweet)

C. bypoleucus *syn* bypoglaucus or C. orbiculatus *syn* C. articulatus

Habit   Vigorous climber which, when allowed to form a woody frame, will make an interesting flowering and fruiting bonsai.
Compost   Code 4.
Position   Part-shade or sun.
Root pruning   Every year for up to five years, then every two.
Wiring   During the growing season.
Propagation   Seed or cutting.
Pests   Scale insect.
Diseases   Mainly trouble-free.

CERCIS (Judas Tree)

The cercis is a small tree with pea-shaped flowers and attractive leaves.

Cercis chinensis

Habit   Bright pink flowers, although leaves can be large. Not recommended for cold climates.
Compost   Code 4.
Position   Sun or part-shade.
Root pruning   March.
Wiring   March.
Propagation   Seed.
Pests   Mainly trouble-free.
Diseases   Mainly trouble-free.

Cercis siliquastrum (Judas tree)

Habit   Will like warmer areas of the garden, bears rosy-lilac flowers.
Compost   Code 4.
Position   Sun or part-shade.
Root pruning   March–April.
Wiring   March.
Propagation   Seed.
Pests   Mainly trouble-free.
Diseases   Mainly trouble-free.

Styles for the Judas Tree

Chokkan   Formal upright or straight-trunk style.
Moyogi   Curving or informal upright trunk.
Shakan   Leaning or slanting trunk.
Bankan   Twisted trunk, coiled almost like a spring.
So-kan   Double trunk which divides close to the base of the trunk.
Kabudachi   Multiple trunk – single tree at the base, splitting into several trunks to form a group.
Hokidachi   Broom style, the head or foliage is shaped like a broom.
Fukinagashi   Windswept style – all the branches lean in one direction.
Neagari   Exposed root system.

CHAENOMELES (Japanese quince)

Chaenomeles japonica (Maule's flowering quince)

Chaenomeles lagenaria (flowering quince)

Chaenomeles sinensis (Chinese quince)

Habit All the above varieties flower and fruit.
Compost Code 4.
Position Part-shade or sun.
Root pruning Every year for up to five years, then every two.
Wiring During the growing season.
Propagation Seed, cutting or grafting.
Pests Aphids.
Diseases Mainly trouble-free.

Chamaecyparis. One of the many bonsai grown by a dedicated Scottish grower.

CHAMAECYPARIS (False Cypress)

Chamaecyparis obtusa (Hinoki cypress)

Habit Bright green foliage, cones are produced in time.
Compost Code 3.
Position Part-shade or sun.
Root pruning Every year for up to five years, then every two.
Wiring In the autumn.
Propagation Seed or cutting.
Pests Mainly trouble-free.
Diseases Mainly trouble-free.

CORNUS

Small flowering *Cornus mas* suitable for bonsai is commonly known as the Cornelian cherry. It makes a delightful bonsai, exposing its bright yellow flowers on bare branches during late winter months. The fruits are red and resemble those of a bonsai crab apple.

Artistic bonsai (*Chamaecyparis*) grown from nursery stock. Note the *Jin*.

[126]

Styles for the Cornus

Chokkan Formal upright or straight-trunk style.
Moyogi Curving or informal upright trunk.
Shakan Leaning or slanting trunk.
So-kan Double trunk which divides close to the base of the trunk.
Kabudachi Multiple trunk – single tree at the base, splitting into several trunks to form a group.
Hokidachi Broom style, the head or foliage is shaped like a broom.
Fukinagashi Windswept style – all the branches lean in one direction.
Neagari Exposed root system.

Cornus chinensis

Habit Deciduous veined leaves. Produces

This eight-year-old *Cornus mas* or Cornelian cherry was grown from garden centre stock and measures 48cm (19in).

yellow flowers in winter, requires good protection from the elements.
Compost Code 4, but will do well in most composts.
Position Sun or part-shade.
Root pruning March–April, every year for up to five years, then every two.
Wiring Will form a block shape if trained from bud pinching, therefore wire during the growing season and remove after six months.
Propagation Seeds or hardwood cuttings in November.
Pests Caterpillars
Diseases Die-back.

Cornus mas (Cornelian cherry)

Habit Deciduous, slow-growing. Forms a net of thick crossing branches.
Compost Code 4, but will do well in most composts.
Position Sun or part-shade.
Root pruning March–April, every year for up to five years, then every two.
Wiring Will form a block shape if trained from bud pinching, therefore wire during the growing season and remove after six months.
Propagation Seeds or hardwood cuttings in November.
Pests Caterpillars.
Diseases Die-back.

COTONEASTER

Cotoneaster horizontalis

Habit Spreading, with herring-bone branch system. Red fruits.
Compost Code 4.
Position Part-shade or sun.
Root pruning Every year for up to five years, then every two.
Wiring During the growing season.
Propagation Seed or cutting.
Pests Mainly trouble-free.
Diseases Mainly trouble-free.

Styles for the Cotoneaster

Chokkan Formal upright or straight-trunk style.
Moyogi Curving or informal upright trunk.
Shakan Leaning or slanting trunk.
Bankan Twisted trunk, coiled almost like a spring.
So-kan Double trunk which divides close to the base of the trunk.

CRATAEGUS (Hawthorn)

Crataegus monogyna is the common hawthorn which is sometimes called the May tree and is one of my favourite bonsai trees. It is a good tree if you are just starting to use more advanced bonsai techniques. It bears fragrant flowers in May, followed by fruits in the autumn. Being very hardy, it will stand up to most cold conditions found in different regions of the world.

Hawthorn collected from the wild.

Crataegus monogyna (hawthorn)

Habit Deciduous. Slow-growing, with thick crossing branches.
Compost Code 5, but will tolerate a wide range of composts.

Styles for the Hawthorn

Chokkan Formal upright or straight-trunk style.
Moyogi Curving or informal upright trunk.
Shakan Leaning or slanting trunk.
Bankan Twisted trunk, coiled almost like a spring.
So-kan Double trunk which divides close to the base of the trunk.
Kabudachi Multiple trunk – single tree at the base, splitting into several trunks to form a group.
Hokidachi Broom style, the head or foliage is shaped like a broom.
Fukinagashi Windswept style – all the branches lean in one direction.
Neagari Exposed root system.
Netsuranari Connecting-root style – an odd number of trees growing from the same root system.
Ishitsuki Tree or trees grown on a rock.
Ikadabuki Raft style – the trunk leans on its side and the branches are only allowed to develop on one side, giving the illusion of several trees growing in a clump.
Yose-ue Group planting which resembles a forest.

Position Sun or part-shade.
Root pruning March–April, every year for up to five years, then every two.
Wiring March and during the growing season, remove wire after six months.
Propagation Air-layering, simple layering, seed or grafting.
Pests Mainly trouble-free.
Diseases Mildew.

The hawthorn is ideal for trying out more advanced bonsai techniques.

CRYPTOMERIA (Japanese Cedar)

Cryptomeria japonica

Habit   Soft green foliage turning russet during the autumn.
Compost   Code 4.
Position   Part-shade or sun.
Root pruning   Every year for up to five years, then every two.
Wiring   During the growing season.
Propagation   Seed or cutting.
Pests   Mainly trouble-free.
Diseases   Mainly trouble-free.

ELAEAGNUS

Elaeagnus commutata (silver berry)

Habit   Leaves are silver and egg-shaped fruits are formed.
Compost   Code 4.
Position   Part-shade or sun.
Root pruning   Every year for up to five years, then every two.
Wiring   During the growing season.

Styles for the Japanese Cedar

Chokkan   Formal upright or straight-trunk style.
Moyogi   Curving or informal upright trunk.
Shakan   Leaning or slanting trunk.
So-kan   Double trunk which divides close to the base of the trunk.
San-kan   Triple trunk.
Go-kan   Five trunks.
Kabudachi   Multiple trunk – single tree at the base, splitting into several trunks to form a group.
Han-kengai   Semi-cascade.
Kengai   Cascade.
Neagari   Exposed root system.
Ishitsuki   Tree or trees planted on a rock.

Styles for the Elaeagnus

Chokkan   Formal upright or straight-trunk style.
Moyogi   Curving or informal upright trunk.
Shakan   Leaning or slanting trunk.
Bankan   Twisted trunk, coiled almost like a spring.
So-kan   Double trunk which divides close to the base of the trunk.
San-kan   Triple trunk.
Go-kan   Five trunks.
Kabudachi   Multiple trunk – single tree at the base, splitting into several trunks to form a group.
Han-kengai   Semi-cascade.
Kengai   Cascade.
Neagari   Exposed root system.
Ishitsuki   Tree or trees planted on a rock.

Propagation   Seed, cutting, or grafting.
Pests   Mainly trouble-free.
Diseases   Mainly trouble-free.

EUONYMUS (Spindle Tree)

Habit   Many forms of euonymus can be used in bonsai but *E. fortunei* and *E. japonicus* are recommended.
Compost   Code 4.
Position   Part-shade or sun.
Root pruning   Every year for up to five years, then every two.
Wiring   During the growing season.
Propagation   Seed or division.
Pests   Mainly trouble-free.
Diseases   Mainly trouble-free.

Japanese white beech can look very attractive during the winter, because of the silvery colour of its bark. The leaves are slightly large.

Styles for the Spindle Tree

Chokkan   Formal upright or straight-trunk style.
Moyogi   Curving or informal upright trunk.
Shakan   Leaning or slanting trunk.
Bankan   Twisted trunk, coiled almost like a spring.
So-kan   Double trunk which divides close to the base of the trunk.
San-kan   Triple trunk.
Go-kan   Five trunks.
Kabudachi   Multiple trunk – single tree at the base, splitting into several trunks to form a group.
Neagari   Exposed root system.
Ishitsuki   Tree or trees planted on a rock.

Both types have fairly large foliage and will need leaf pruning every one or two years. The Japanese beech (*Fagus crenata sieboldii*) is also very popular among bonsai growers.

Fagus crenata (sieboldii)

Habit   Obovate leaves.
Compost   Code 4 or 5, likes lime conditions.
Position   Sun or shade.
Root pruning   March–April, every year for up to five years, then every two.
Wiring   March.
Propagation   Seed.
Pests   Scale insects.
Diseases   Mainly trouble-free.

Fagus sylvatica and Fagus sylvatica 'Riversii'

Habit   Deciduous. Slow-growing; a deep pot is preferable to accommodate root system.

FAGUS (Beech)

A favourite among many people collecting English bonsai. *Fagus sylvatica* is the common form of beech and widely used in bonsai, but there are other forms of beech; *Fagus sylvatica* 'Riversii', for example, has dark purple leaves.

[130]

Styles for the Beech

Chokkan   Formal upright or straight-trunk style.
Moyogi   Curving or informal upright trunk.
Shakan   Leaning or slanting trunk.
So-kan   Double trunk which divides close to the base of the trunk.
Kabudachi   Multiple trunk – single tree at the base, splitting into several trunks to form a group.
Hokidachi   Broom style, the head or foliage is shaped like a broom.
Fukinagashi   Windswept style – all the branches lean in one direction.
Neagari   Exposed root system.
Netsuranari   Connecting-root style – an odd number of trees growing from the same root system.
Ikadabuki   Raft style – the trunk leans on its side and the branches are only allowed to develop on one side, giving the illusion of several trees growing in a clump.
Yose-ue   Group planting which resembles a forest.

A beautiful specimen of a beech, collected from the wild. This photograph was taken at a show.

White beech grown from nursery stock.

Compost   Code 4 or 5. Likes compost with a low peat content and well drained.
Position   Sun or part-shade.
Root pruning   March–April, every year for up to five years, then every two.
Wiring   March.
Propagation   Seed or grafting.
Pests   Scale insects.
Diseases   Canker, die-back.

FORSYTHIA

The forsythia will make an excellent spring flowering bonsai. The flowers are a bright yellow and are grown on new wood.

Forsythia europaea (European golden ball)

Habit   Pale yellow flowers.
Compost   Code 4.
Position   Sun or part-shade.

Root pruning Early March. Allow time to recover before flowering.
Wiring December–early March.
Propagation Cuttings.
Pests Mainly trouble-free.
Diseases Mainly trouble-free.

Styles for the Forsythia

Chokkan Formal upright or straight-trunk style.
Moyogi Curving or informal upright trunk.
Shakan Leaning or slanting trunk.
Bankan Twisted trunk, coiled almost like a spring.
So-kan Double trunk which divides close to the base of the trunk.
Hokidachi Broom style, the head or foliage is shaped like a broom.
Fukinagashi Windswept style – all the branches lean in one direction.
Neagari Exposed root system.
Ishitsuki Tree or trees grown on a rock.

Forsythia ovata

Habit Early-flowering, small form of forsythia.
Compost Code 4.
Position Sun or part-shade.
Root pruning Early March, before flowering.
Wiring December–March.
Propagation Cuttings.
Pests Mainly trouble-free.
Diseases Mainly trouble-free.

Forsythia suspensa

Habit Small rambling or climbing form of forsythia.
Compost Code 4.
Position Sun or part-shade.
Root pruning February, before flowering.
Wiring December–March.
Propagation Cuttings.
Pests Mainly trouble-free.
Diseases Mainly trouble-free.

Forsythia virdissima 'Bronxensis'

Habit Dense, compact forsythia with a network of fine twiggy branches.
Compost Code 4.
Position Sun or shade.
Root pruning Early March.
Wiring December–March.
Propagation Cuttings.
Pests Mainly trouble-free.
Diseases Mainly trouble-free.

FRAXINUS (Ash)

Very hardy and will tolerate most cold winters. *Fraxinus excelsior* is the common ash, easily recognized by its black buds in winter. The leaves are pinnate and tend to be slightly large for the tree. Other forms such as *Fraxinus excelsior* 'Nana', which is more of a bush than a tree, and *Fraxinus excelsior* 'Erosa', a small tree with a narrow-shaped leaf, make excellent bonsai. Flowering forms such as *Fraxinus floribunda* bear large white flowers.

Ash group grown from random seed sowing.

Fraxinus excelsior (common ash)

Habit Deciduous, hardy fast-growing tree. 'Nana' and 'Erosa' varieties are slow-growing.
Compost Code 5 or 4.
Position Sun or part-shade.
Root pruning March–April, every year for up to ten years, then every two.
Wiring During growing season. Cover wire to protect bark, remove after six months.
Propagation Seed.
Pests Mainly trouble-free.
Diseases Mainly trouble-free.

Styles for the Ash Tree

Chokkan Formal upright or straight-trunk style.
Moyogi Curving or informal upright trunk.
Shakan Leaning or slanting trunk.
Bankan Twisted trunk, coiled almost like a spring.
So-kan Double trunk which divides close to the base of the trunk.
Kabudachi Multiple trunk – single tree at the base, splitting into several trunks to form a group.
Fukinagashi Windswept style – all the branches lean in one direction.
Neagari Exposed root system.

FUSCHIA

Habit Many forms of fuschia can be grown as outdoor and indoor bonsai. However, the smaller plants should be used as *F*. 'Tom Thumb' or *F*. 'Mrs Popple'.
Compost Code 3.
Position Part-shade or sun.
Root pruning Every year for up to five years, then every two.
Wiring During the growing season.
Propagation Seed or cutting.
Pests Aphids.
Diseases Mildew.

Styles for the Fuschia

Hokidachi Broom.
Kengai Cascade.
Neagari Exposed root system.
Ishitsuki Tree or trees planted on a rock.

A very old specimen of a ginkgo, imported from China.

GLEDITSIA

Gleditsia Triacanthos (honey locust)

Habit Pinnate green leaves, branches contain spines.
Compost Code 3.
Position Part-shade or sun.
Root pruning Every year for up to five years, then every two.
Wiring During the growing season.
Propagation Seed.
Pests Mainly trouble-free.
Diseases Mainly trouble-free.

[133]

Styles for the Gleditsia

Chokkan Formal upright or straight-trunk style.
Moyogi Curving or informal upright trunk.
Shakan Leaning or slanting trunk.
Bankan Twisted trunk, coiled almost like a spring.
Neagari Exposed root system.
Ishitsuki Tree or trees planted on a rock.

ILEX (Holly)

Ilex crenata (Japanese holly)

Upright shrub with black fruits.

Ilex sieboldii (deciduous holly)

Habit Compact shrub with red fruits.
Compost Code 4.
Position Part-shade or sun.
Root pruning Every year for up to five years, then every two.
Wiring During the growing season.
Propagation Seed or cutting.
Pests Mainly trouble-free.
Diseases Mainly trouble-free.

Styles for the Holly

Chokkan Formal upright or straight-trunk style.
Moyogi Curving or informal upright trunk.
Shakan Leaning or slanting trunk.
Bankan Twisted trunk, coiled almost like a spring.
So-kan Double trunk which divides close to the base of the trunk.
San-kan Triple trunk.
Kabudachi Multiple trunk – single tree at the base, splitting into several trunks to form a group.

JASMINUM (Winter Flowering Jasmine)

Although the jasmine is grown as a climbing plant it will, after forming a woody framework of trunk and branches, make an excellent late-winter flowering bonsai. The flowers, like those of the forsythia, are produced on new wood.

Jasminum nudiflorum

Habit Bright yellow flowers from November to February.
Compost Code 4.
Position Sun or shade.
Root pruning March, after flowering.
Wiring March–April, but only on woody section and not young green growth.
Propagation Cuttings or layering.
Pests Mainly trouble-free.
Diseases Mainly trouble-free.

Styles for the Jasmine

Chokkan Formal upright or straight-trunk style.
Moyogi Curving or informal upright trunk.
Shakan Leaning or slanting trunk.
Bankan Twisted trunk, coiled almost like a spring.
So-kan Double trunk which divides close to the base of the trunk.
Kabudachi Multiple trunk – single tree at the base, splitting into several trunks to form a group.
Hokidachi Broom style, the head or foliage is shaped like a broom.
Fukinagashi Windswept style – all the branches lean in one direction.
Neagari Exposed root system.
Netsuranari Connecting-root style – an odd number of trees growing from the same root system.
Ishitsuki Tree or trees grown on a rock.
Ikadabuki Raft style – the trunk leans on its side and the branches are only allowed to develop on one side, giving the impression of several trees growing in a clump.

JUNIPERUS

See Chapter 9.

Juniper side by side with a rock (not to be confused with planting over rock).

LABURNUM (Golden Rain)

Small yellow flowering tree. It will make an excellent bonsai, blooming in late spring to early summer. *Laburnum leguminosae* is the common laburnum and great care should be taken to keep the seeds, which are poisonous, away from children.

Laburnum leguminosae (golden rain or golden shower)

Habit   Deciduous. Small, slow-growing tree.
Compost   Code 4.
Position   Sun or part-shade.
Root pruning   March–April, every two years.
Wiring   March. Cover wire to protect bark, remove after six months.

Propagation   Seed or hardwood cutting in November.
Pests   Mainly trouble-free.
Diseases   Mainly trouble-free.

Styles for the Laburnum

Chokkan   Formal upright or straight-trunk style.
Moyogi   Curving or informal upright trunk.
Shakan   Leaning or slanting trunk.
So-kan   Double trunk which divides close to the base of the trunk.
Kabudachi   Multiple trunk – single tree at the base, splitting into several trunks to form a group.
Han-kengai   Semi-cascade.
Kengai   Cascade.
Hokidachi   Broom style, the head or foliage is shaped like a broom.
Fukinagashi   Windswept style – all the branches lean in one direction.
Neagari   Exposed root system.
Ishitsuki   Tree or trees grown on a rock.

LARIX (Larch)

Larix decidua (European larch)

Sheds needles in winter.

Larix leptolepis (Japanese larch)

Habit   Horizontal branches; again sheds its needles in winter.
Compost   Code 4.
Position   Part-shade or sun.
Root pruning   Every year for up to five years, then every two.
Wiring   During the growing season.
Propagation   Seed or cutting.
Pests   Mainly trouble-free.
Diseases   Mainly trouble-free.

[135]

Styles for the Larch

Chokkan   Formal upright or straight-trunk style.
Moyogi   Curving or informal upright trunk.
Shakan   Leaning or slanting trunk.
Bankan   Twisted trunk, coiled almost like a spring.
So-kan   Double trunk which divides close to the base of the trunk.
San-kan   Triple trunk.

Go-kan   Five trunks.
Kabudachi   Multiple trunk – single tree at the base, splitting into several trunks to form a group.
Han-kengai   Semi-cascade.
Kengai   Cascade.
Neagari   Exposed root system.
Ishitsuki   Tree or trees planted on a rock.

LONICERA (Honeysuckle)

Habit   Many forms of Lonicera will make bonsai although the flower tends to be on the large side. A framework to build a woody trunk and main branches are the most important points when first starting.
Compost   Code 4.
Position   Part-shade or sun.
Root pruning   Every year for up to five years, then every two.
Wiring   During the growing season.
Propagation   Seed, cutting or layering.
Pests   Aphids.
Diseases   Mildew.

Styles for the Honeysuckle

Chokkan   Formal upright or straight-trunk style.
Moyogi   Curving or informal upright trunk.
Shakan   Leaning or slanting trunk.
Bankan   Twisted trunk, coiled almost like a spring.
Neagari   Exposed root system.
Ishitsuki   Tree or trees planted on a rock.

MALUS (Flowering Crab Apple)

Small, very hardy, flowering crab apple. Produces small cherry-like apples in the autumn. The leaves and flowers tend to look too large for the tree and will not respond to leaf pruning like other bonsai. *Malus floribunda* or Japanese crab, is the most widely used crab in bonsai and produces white flowers early in the spring, followed by red and yellow fruits in the autumn.

Malus floribunda or Japanese crab apple flowers in spring, followed by fruits in the autumn.

Malus floribunda (Japanese crab apple)

Habit Deciduous. Small, slow-growing tree.
Compost Code 5.
Position Sun or part-shade.
Root pruning March. Every year for up to ten years, then every two.
Wiring March. Cover wire to protect bark and remove after six months.
Propagation Budding, grafting and seed.
Pests Aphids, caterpillars.
Diseases Canker, coral spot, die-back, fire blight, powdery mildew.

Styles for the Crab Apple

Chokkan Formal upright or straight-trunk style.
Moyogi Curving or informal upright trunk.
Shakan Leaning or slanting trunk.
Bankan Twisted trunk, coiled almost like a spring.
Hokidachi Broom style, the head or foliage is shaped like a broom.
Fukinagashi Windswept style – all the branches lean in one direction.
Neagari Exposed root system.
Ishitsuki Tree or trees grown on a rock.

MORUS (Mulberries)

This small slow-growing tree, *Morus alba* or the white mulberry, produces a white fruit which turns to a pinkish-red colour. Although found in China and introduced into this country in the fifteenth century, it has long become an old prized British tree.

Morus nigra, the black mulberry, has a wide spreading top growth and thick, gnarled, old-looking trunk. *Morus rubra* commonly known as the red mulberry is very hard to find in local garden centres and nurseries. *Morus nana* is the slow-growing dwarf form with very compact top growth which needs constant thinning.

Styles for the Mulberries

Chokkan Formal upright or straight-trunk style.
Moyogi Curving or informal upright trunk.
Shakan Leaning or slanting trunk.
Bankan Twisted trunk, coiled almost like a spring.
So-kan Double trunk which divides close to the base of the trunk.
Kabudachi Multiple trunk – single tree at the base, splitting into several trunks to form a group.
Hokidachi Broom style, the head or foliage is shaped like a broom.
Fukinagashi Windswept style – all the branches lean in one direction.
Neagari Exposed root system.
Netsuranari Connecting-root style – an odd number of trees growing from the same root system.
Ikadabuki Raft style – the trunk leans on its side and the branches are only allowed to develop on one side, giving the impression of several trees growing in a clump.
Ishitsuki Tree or trees grown on a rock.

Morus alba, M. nana and M. rubra (mulberries)

Habit Deciduous. Slow-growing.
Compost Code 3. Open, well-drained compost.
Position Sun or part-shade.
Root pruning March–April, every year for up to five years, then every two.
Wiring March. Remove wire after six months.
Propagation Seed, hardwood cuttings in November.
Pests Caterpillars.
Diseases Mildew.

MYRTUS

See Chapter 9.

NANDINA

See Chapter 9.

NOTHOFAGUS (Beech)

A fast-growing tree, will make a very attractive bonsai. Commonly known as the Antarctic beech, it has small, rounded heart-shaped leaves which turn to yellow during the autumn fall.

Styles for the Beech

Chokkan   Formal upright or straight-trunk style.
Moyogi   Curving or informal upright trunk.
Shakan   Leaning or slanting trunk.
So-kan   Double trunk which divides close to the base of the trunk.
Kabudachi   Multiple trunk – single tree at the base, splitting into several trunks to form a group.
Hokidachi   Broom style, the head or foliage is shaped like a broom.
Fukinagashi   Windswept style – all the branches lean in one direction.
Neagari   Exposed root system.
Netsuranari   Connecting-root style – an odd number of trees growing from the same root system.
Ikadabuki   Raft style – the trunk leans on its side and the branches are only allowed to develop on one side, giving the illusion of several trees growing in a clump.
Yose-ue   Group planting which resembles a forest.

Nothofagus antarctica

Habit   Deciduous. Fast-growing, will make an excellent bonsai in a short space of time.
Compost   Code 3; dislikes too much lime.
Position   Sun or part-shade.
Root pruning   March–April, every year for up to five years, then every two.
Wiring   During the growing season. Cover wire to protect bark, check wire after two months and remove after six months.
Propagation   Air-layering, cuttings and seed.
Pests   Mainly trouble-free.

Diseases   Mainly trouble-free.

See also Chapter 9, under 'Nothofagus'.

PICEA (Spruce)

Picea jezonensis (Jezo or Hondo spruce)

Habit   Green foliage, silver on the underside.
Compost   Code 4.
Position   Part-shade or sun.
Root pruning   Every year for up to five years, then every two.
Wiring   Autumn.
Propagation   Seed or cutting.
Pests   Mainly trouble-free.
Diseases   Mainly trouble-free.

Styles for the Spruce

Chokkan   Formal upright or straight-trunk style.
Moyogi   Curving or informal upright trunk.
Shakan   Leaning or slanting trunk.
Bankan   Twisted trunk, coiled almost like a spring.
So-kan   Double trunk which divides close to the base of the trunk.
San-kan   Triple trunk.
Go-kan   Five trunks.
Kabudachi   Multiple trunk – single tree at the base, splitting into several trunks to form a group.
Han-kengai   Semi-cascade.
Kengai   Cascade.
Neagari   Exposed root system.
Ishitsuki   Tree or trees planted on a rock.

PINUS

See Chapter 7, pages 91–96.

Japanese white pine grafted on to the rootstock of a black pine – you can see the graft at the base of the foliage.

Wiring During the growing season. Remove wire after six months.
Propagation Hardwood cuttings in November.
Pests Mainly trouble-free.
Diseases Mainly trouble-free.

Styles for the Poplar

Chokkan Formal upright or straight-trunk style.
Moyogi Curving or informal upright trunk.
Shakan Leaning or slanting trunk.
So-kan Double trunk which divides close to the base of the trunk.
Kabudachi Multiple trunk – single tree at the base, splitting into several trunks to form a group.
Hokidachi Broom style, the head or foliage is shaped like a broom.
Fukinagashi Windswept style – all the branches lean in one direction.
Neagari Exposed root system.

POMEGRANATE

See Chapter 9, under 'Pomegranate'.

POPULUS (Poplar)

There are many forms of poplar throughout Europe which can be trained quite successfully into bonsai trees given the time. *Populus alba* is the white poplar, because of the white underside of the leaves which turn yellow in the autumn. *Populus nigra* is commonly called the black poplar, and *Populus tremula* 'Pendula' the weeping poplar or weeping aspen.

Populus alba, P. nigra and P. tremula 'Pendula'

Habit Deciduous.
Compost Code 4.
Position Sun or shade.
Root pruning Every year for up to ten years, then every two.

PRUNUS (Flowering Cherry)

The common names are wild cherry or gean, which can be trained quite easily into an attractive and colourful flowering bonsai. The smooth grey bark will turn red with age and peel with some forms of prunus. The flowers which blossom in April are white and are followed by small red-to-purple fruits.

Prunus avium

Habit Deciduous, slow-growing tree.
Compost Code 4 or 5.
Position Sun or part-shade.
Root pruning March–April, every year for up to five years, then every two.
Wiring March. Cover wire to protect bark, remove after six months.
Propagation Budding, cuttings, grafting and seed.
Pests Mainly trouble-free.
Diseases Canker, die-back.

[139]

Styles for the Prunus

Chokkan Formal upright or straight-trunk style.
Moyogi Curving or informal upright trunk.
Shakan Leaning or slanting trunk.
Bankan Twisted trunk, coiled almost like a spring.
So-kan Double trunk which divides close to the base of the trunk.
San-kan Triple trunk.
Go-kan Five trunks.
Kabudachi Multiple trunk – single tree at the base, splitting into several trunks to form a group.
Han-kengai Semi-cascade.
Kengai Cascade.
Neagari Exposed root system.
Ishitsuki Tree or trees planted on a rock.

Prunus incisa 'Thumb' (Japanese dwarf cherry)

Habit Bears droopy flowers.
Compost Code 4.
Position Part-shade.
Root pruning Every year for up to five years, then every two.
Wiring During the growing season.
Propagation Seed, cutting or grafting.
Pests Aphids, caterpillars.
Diseases Canker.

The species of this prunus is uncertain, but it is of a weeping, flowered variety.

PYRACANTHA (Firethorn)

Pyracantha angustifolia

Habit   Spreading habit; semi-evergreen fruits in the autumn.
Compost   Code 4.
Position   Part-shade or sun.
Root pruning   Every year for up to five years, then every two.
Wiring   During the growing season.
Propagation   Seed or cutting.
Pests   Mainly trouble-free.
Diseases   Mainly trouble-free.

Styles for the Firethorn

Chokkan   Formal upright or straight-trunk style.
Moyogi   Curving or informal upright trunk.
Shakan   Leaning or slanting trunk.
Bankan   Twisted trunk, coiled almost like a spring.
So-kan   Double trunk which divides close to the base of the trunk.
San-kan   Triple trunk.
Go-kan   Five trunks.
Kabudachi   Multiple trunk – single tree at the base, splitting into several trunks to form a group.
Han-kengai   Semi-cascade.
Kengai   Cascade.
Neagari   Exposed root system.
Ishitsuki   Tree or trees planted on a rock.

QUERCUS (Oak)

The oak tree can, if given time, form into a small, mighty version of the magnificent specimens seen in the British countryside. However, oaks are not the best subjects to train as bonsai. The leaves of the oak tend to be too large and even with pruning techniques, you cannot guarantee a smaller leaf. The oak will in most cases only live for short periods. I have grown some successfully for ten to fifteen years, only to find them die overnight even though they had been given careful attention. Oaks planted in deep bonsai pots seem to have a better survival rate than those planted in shallow pots.

Common oak (*Quercus robur*)   English oak, hardy and slow-growing.
Cork oak (*Quercus suber*)   Bark corky.
Holm oak (*Quercus ilex*)   Evergreen oak originating from Mediterranean regions.
Red oak (*Quercus rubra*)   Leaves start green, then turn red before autumn.
White oak (*Quercus alba*)   Good autumn colour.
Willow oak (*Quercus phellos*)   Willow-like leaves.

Styles for the Oak

Chokkan   Formal upright or straight-trunk style.
Moyogi   Curving or informal upright trunk.
Shakan   Leaning or slanting trunk.
Bankan   Twisted trunk, coiled almost like a spring.
Hokidachi   Broom style, the head or foliage is shaped like a broom.
Fukinagashi   Windswept style – all the branches lean in one direction.
Neagari   Exposed root system.

Most Oaks

Habit   Slow-growing, large leaves.
Compost   Code 5.
Position   Sun or part-shade.
Root pruning   March–April, every year for up to ten years, then every two.
Wiring   Try to shape by bud pruning. Otherwise, wire during the growing season and remove after six months.
Propagation   Sow seeds in pots or a prepared plot in the garden during the autumn (*see* Chapter 3).
Pests   Mainly trouble-free.
Diseases   Mildew, gall.

RHODODENDRON ARBOREUM (Rhododendron)

Both Rhododendron and Azalea are linked to the same family, *Ericaceae*, and the majority tend to be classed as shrubs rather than trees. *Rhododendron arboreum*, however, forms into a small tree and is suitable for a large, soil-grown, specimen bonsai. In areas where the soil has a high lime content, it is best to grow the specimen in training boxes, since the tree will not survive in a compost or a soil that contains lime.

See Chapter 9 for less hardy forms of rhododendrons and azaleas.

Rhododendron arboreum, R. a. 'Album', R. a. 'Blood Red' and R. a. 'Roseum'

Habit   Fairly slow-growing.
Compost   Code 2.
Position   Part-shade. Dislikes frost, 'Blood Red' especially.
Root pruning   Every two years when grown in soil and boxes, then every year for up to five years when grown in large bonsai pot. From then on, every two to three years.
Wiring   During the growing season. Cover wire to protect bark, remove after six months.
Propagation   Seed, cuttings, layering and agrafting.
Pests   Rhododendron bug.
Diseases   Chlorosis, azalea gall.

ROBINIA (Common Acacia) 'False Acacia' and 'Black Locust'

Robinia pseudoacacia can be shaped into a colourful, white flowering, slightly scented bonsai. The rugged bark is an extra bonus.

Robinia pseudoacacia

Habit   Slow-growing.
Compost   Code 3 or 4.

Styles for the Acacia

Chokkan   Formal upright or straight-trunk style.
Moyogi   Curving or informal upright trunk.
Shakan   Leaning or slanting trunk.
Bankan   Twisted trunk, coiled almost like a spring.
So-kan   Double trunk which divides close to the base of the trunk.
Hokidachi   Broom style, the head or foliage is shaped like a broom.
Fukinagashi   Windswept style – all the branches lean in one direction.
Neagari   Exposed root system.
Ishitsuki   Tree or trees grown on a rock.

Position   Sun or shade.
Root pruning   March–April. Every year for up to five years, then every two.
Wiring   March. Remove wire after six months.
Propagation   Seed, grafting during March, root cuttings taken between December and January.
Pests   Mainly trouble-free.
Diseases   Mainly trouble-free.

SALIX (Willow)

Willows range from large weeping trees to small groundcover shrubs. Willows are recognized and accepted when cut back hard ('pollarded') and, therefore, bonsai can be modelled on the natural shapes found in the wild. However, certain forms are more suited than others.

Salix caprea or goat willow or pussy willow   Bears silver catkins which turn to yellow. The stems lend themselves quite readily to bending and shaping with wire, but care should be taken and the wire covered to protect the young soft bark.

Salix caprea 'Pendula'   The weeping form of willow. Because it is grafted at the top, or 'top-worked', it is better for the beginner to purchase a young tree from a nursery or garden centre which will sell such trees from about 45cm (18in) in height and therefore make ideal starting material.

Salix, commonly known as willow, is very easy to propagate.

Salix repens or creeping willow This is more of a shrub than a tree with its creeping habit. It is ideal for a cascading bonsai. There are many creeping forms which you may use, such as *Salix argentea*, which will need a moist and sandy compost such as a code 3; *Salix repens subopposita* 'Voorthuizen;' with very small catkins; *Salix reticulata*, which again likes a moist open compost.

All Salix

Habit Fast-growing, ages quickly. Upright, weeping and cascade.
Compost Code 3 for most weeping willows and code 4 for all others.
Position Sun or shade.
Root pruning March–April. Every year for up to five years, then every two.
Wiring March. Cover wire to protect bark and remove after six months.
Propagation Very easy from hardwood cuttings taken during November.
Pests Caterpillars.
Diseases Die-back, mildew.

SEQUOIA

Sequoiadendron giganteum (Sequoia gigantea or Sequoia wellingtonia)

Habit Wellingtonia also known as the 'Mammoth Tree' has an interesting bark. The leaves are bright green, pointed and prickly.
Compost Code 4.
Position Part-shade or sun.
Root pruning Every year for up to five years, then every two.
Wiring During the growing season.
Propagation Seed.
Pests Mainly trouble-free.
Diseases Mainly trouble-free.

Styles for the Willow

Chokkan Formal upright or straight-trunk style.
Moyogi Curving or informal upright trunk.
Shakan Leaning or slanting trunk.
Bankan Twisted trunk, coiled almost like a spring.
So-kan Double trunk which divides close to the base of the trunk.
Kabudachi Multiple trunk – single tree at the base, splitting into several trunks to form a group.
Hokidachi Broom style, the head or foliage is shaped like a broom.
Fukinagashi Windswept style – all the branches lean in one direction.
Neagari Exposed root system.
Netsuranari Connecting-root style, an odd number of trees growing from the same root system.
Ishitsuki Tree or trees grown on a rock.
Ikadabuki Raft style – the tree leans on its side, and the branches are only allowed to develop on one side, giving the impression of several trunks growing together.

Styles for the Sequoia

Chokkan Formal upright or straight-trunk style.
Neagari Exposed root system.

SORBUS

Sorbus aucuparia (mountain ash or rowan)

Habit   Pinnate leaves, bright red fruits during the autumn.
Compost   Code 4.
Position   Part-shade or sun.
Root pruning   Every year for up to five years, then every two.
Wiring   During the growing season.
Propagation   Seed.
Pests   Mainly trouble-free.
Diseases   Mainly trouble-free.

Pests   Mainly trouble-free.
Diseases   Mainly trouble-free.

Mature *Stewartia* group in early spring.

Styles for the Mountain Ash

Chokkan   Formal upright or straight-trunk style.
Moyogi   Curving or informal upright trunk.
Shakan   Leaning or slanting trunk.
Bankan   Twisted trunk, coiled almost like a spring.
So-kan   Double trunk which divides close to the base of the trunk.
San-kan   Triple trunk.
Neagari   Exposed root system.
Ishitsuki   Tree or trees planted on a rock.

STEWARTIA (Stuartia)

Stewartia monadelpha or Stewartia koreana

Habit   Attractive bark which flakes, adding interest to the bonsai.
Compost   Code 2 with extra grit.
Position   Part-shade or sun.
Root pruning   Every year for up to five years, then every two.
Wiring   During the growing season.
Propagation   Seed or cutting.

Styles for the Stuartia

Chokkan   Formal upright or straight-trunk style.
Moyogi   Curving or informal upright trunk.
Shakan   Leaning or slanting trunk.
Bankan   Twisted trunk, coiled almost like a spring.
So-kan   Double trunk which divides close to the base of the trunk.
San-kan   Triple trunk.
Go-kan   Five trunks.
Kabudachi   Multiple trunk – single tree at the base, splitting into several trunks to form a group.
Han-kengai   Semi-cascade.
Neagari   Exposed root system.
Ishitsuki   Tree or trees planted on a rock.

TAMARIX (Tamarisk)

Tamarix gallica (common tamarisk)

Tamarix parviflora (Tetrandra purpurea)

Habit Tamarix has slender branches and bears plume-like foliage.
Compost Code 4.
Position Part-shade or sun.
Root pruning Every year for up to five years, then every two.
Wiring During the growing season.
Propagation Seed.
Pests Mainly trouble-free.
Diseases Mainly trouble-free.

Styles for the Tamarisk

Chokkan Formal upright or straight-trunk style.
Bankan Twisted trunk, coiled almost like a spring.
San-kan Triple trunk.
Go-kan Five trunks.
Kabudachi Multiple trunk – single tree at the base, splitting into several trunks to form a group.
Ishitsuki Tree or trees planted on a rock.

TAXUS (Yew)

Taxus baccata (English yew)

Evergreen with fruits.

Taxus cuspidata (Japanese yew)

Habit Leaves are broader.
Compost Code 4.
Position Part-shade or sun.
Root pruning Every year for up to five years, then every two.
Wiring During the winter months.
Propagation Seed or cutting.
Pests Mainly trouble-free.
Diseases Mainly trouble-free.

Styles for the Yew

Chokkan Formal upright or straight-trunk style.
Moyogi Curving or informal upright trunk.
Shakan Leaning or slanting trunk.
Bankan Twisted trunk, coiled almost like a spring.
So-kan Double trunk which divides close to the base of the trunk.
San-kan Triple trunk.
Go-kan Five trunks.
Kabudachi Multiple trunk – single tree at the base, splitting into several trunks to form a group.

TSUGA (Hemlock)

Tsuga heterophylla (western hemlock)

Spreading branches, white bands beneath leaves.

Tsuga diversifolice (Japanese hemlock)

Habit Hardy evergreen.
Compost Code 4.
Position Part-shade or sun.
Root pruning Every year for up to five years, then every two.
Wiring During the growing season. Avoid young growth.
Propagation Seed or cutting.
Pests Mainly trouble-free.
Diseases Mainly trouble-free.

WISTERIA

Wisteria sinensis (Chinese wisteria)

Bonsai producing flowers in May/June.

Wisteria floribunda (Japanese wisteria)

Habit More scent than *Wisteria sinensis*.
Compost Code 3.
Position Part-shade or sun.
Root pruning Every year for up to five years, then every two.
Wiring During the growing season.
Propagation Seed, layering or grafting.
Pests Aphids.
Diseases Mosaic virus.

ULMUS (Elm)

Ulmus procera *syn* U. campestris (English elm)

Habit Erect tree with mid-green leaves.
Compost Code 4.
Position Part-shade or sun.
Root pruning Every year for up to five years, then every two.
Wiring During the growing season.
Propagation Collect from wild or seed.
Pests Mainly trouble-free.
Diseases Dutch elm.

ZELKOVA (Grey Bark Elm)

Zelkova has been used for many years in bonsai and is probably best known for the broom style (*Hokidachi*).

Wisteria showing new growth after flowering.

[146]

Styles for the Wisteria

Chokkan   Formal upright or straight-trunk style.
Moyogi   Curving or informal upright trunk.
Shakan   Leaning or slanting trunk.
Bankan   Twisted trunk, coiled almost like a spring.
So-kan   Double trunk which divides close to the base of the trunk.
Han-kengai   Semi-cascade.
Kengai   Cascade.

Styles for the Zelkova

Chokkan   Formal upright or straight-trunk style.
Moyogi   Curving or informal upright trunk.
Shakan   Leaning or slanting trunk.
Bankan   Twisted trunk, coiled almost like a spring.
So-kan   Double trunk which divides close to the base of the trunk.
Kabudachi   Multiple trunk – single tree at the base, splitting into several trunks to form a group.
Hokidachi   Broom style, the head or foliage is shaped like a broom.
Fukinagashi   Windswept style – all the branches lean in one direction.
Neagari   Exposed root system.
Netsuranari   Connecting-root style – an odd number of trees.
Ishitsuki   Tree or trees grown on a rock.
Ikadabuki   Raft style – the trunk leans on its side and the branches are only allowed to develop on one side, giving the impression of several trees growing in a clump.
Yose-ue   Group planting which resembles a forest.

Zelkova group showing a network of fine, bare branches during the winter.

Zelkova serrata

Habit   Grey bark, leaves have coarse teeth, autumn colour can either be bronze or red.
Compost   Code 4.
Position   Sun or part-shade.
Root pruning   March–April.
Wiring   March.
Propagation   Seed or cuttings.
Pests   Mainly trouble-free.
Diseases   Mainly trouble-free.

Chapter 9

AN A–Z OF INDOOR BONSAI

Many forms of trees and shrubs from the warmer regions of the world will grow as indoor bonsai in the colder regions, and some hardy trees will grow inside of an open building in the warmer countries. The trees listed in this chapter have been chosen as tried and tested specimens. Although some of the plants listed will never grow into true, woody trees, they will make interesting, artistic and abstract shapes full of charm and grace. Sometimes, additional features such as driftwood and colourful decorative pots will help to give shape and form to the plant.

Position

The obvious position for most indoor bonsai is close to the window. This is fine between late spring and early autumn, but during winter time, bonsai should be removed from the window during the night to avoid frost damage. Central heating and double glazing will not prevent temperatures from dropping in the window area. Never place a bonsai on top of a television: heat canker will form if this rule is not followed.

Styles for the Acacia

Chokkan Formal upright or straight-trunk style.
Moyogi Curving or informal upright trunk.
Shakan Leaning or slanting trunk.
Bankan Twisted trunk, coiled almost like a spring.
So-kan Double trunk which divides close to the base of the trunk.
Hokidachi Broom style, the head or foliage is shaped like a broom.
Fukinagashi Windswept style – all the branches lean in one direction.
Neagari Exposed root system.
Ishitsuki Tree or trees grown on a rock.

Watering Summer: every day; winter: every two to three days.
Root pruning March–April, every year for up to five years old, then every two.
Wiring March.
Propagation Seeds or cuttings. Seed: sow in April in compost Code 1, at a temperature of 16°C (61°F). Cuttings: a young, semi-ripe cutting with a heel taken between the months of April and May, in a compost Code 2 at a temperature between 16–18°C (61–64°F).
Pests Mealybug, caterpillars, red spider mite.
Diseases Wilt, die-back.

Acacia dealbata (mimosa)

Fast-growing tree from Australia which has a silvery, fern-like foliage. It is also known as 'silver wattle'. Globular heads of small, bright yellow

Acacia karoo (acacia)

This yellow-flowering, deciduous tree with its fern-like leaves and white thorns will make an excellent indoor bonsai. Originating from South Africa, it will tolerate the warmer conditions of indoor cultivation.

Compost Code 4.
Position Plenty of light and good ventilation.
Temperature Winter: never below 4°C (39°F).

[148]

flowers grow in clusters along its branches, making for a colourful bonsai.

Compost   Code 4.
Position   Plenty of light and good ventilation.
Temperature   Winter: never below 4°C (39°F), otherwise the acacia will wilt. General temperature between 15–18°C (59–64°F).
Watering   Summer: every day; winter: every two to three days.
Root pruning   Every year for up to five years, then every two.
Wiring   March.
Propagation   Seed or cuttings. Seed: sow in April in a seed compost Code 1, with a temperature of 16°C (61°F). Cuttings: between softwood and semi-ripe with a heel taken between the months of April and May, in compost Code 2, with bottom heat at a temperature of 16–18°C (61–64°F).
Pests   Mealybug and Tortrix caterpillars if placed outside during the summer.
Diseases   Mainly trouble-free.

Styles for the Mimosa

Chokkan   Formal upright or straight-trunk style.
Moyogi   Curving or informal upright trunk.
Shakan   Leaning or slanting trunk.
Bankan   Twisted trunk, coiled almost like a spring.
So-kan   Double trunk which divides close to the base of the trunk.
Kabudachi   Multiple trunk – single tree at the base, splitting into several trunks to form a group.
Hokidachi   Broom style, the head or foliage is shaped like a broom.
Fukinagashi   Windswept style – all the branches lean in one direction.
Neagari   Exposed root system.
Ishitsuki   Tree or trees grown on a rock.

Acacia longifolia (Sydney golden wattle)

Small, shrubby Australian tree with yellow, strongly-scented flowers covering its dense network of branches.

Styles for the Sydney Golden Wattle

Chokkan   Formal upright or straight trunk style.
Moyogi   Curving or informal upright trunk.
Shakan   Leaning or slanting trunk.
Bankan   Twisted trunk, coiled almost like a spring.
So-kan   Double trunk which divides close to the base of the trunk.
Kabudachi   Multiple trunk – single tree at the base, splitting into several trunks to form a group.
Hokidachi   Broom style, the head or foliage is shaped like a broom.
Fukinagashi   Windswept style – all the branches lean in one direction.
Neagari   Exposed root system.
Ishitsuki   Tree or trees grown on a rock.

Compost   Code 4, extra sand.
Position   Plenty of light and good ventilation.
Temperature   Winter: never allow the temperature to drop below 4°C (39°F). Summer: between 15–18°C (59–64°F).
Watering   Summer: every day; winter: every two to three days.
Root pruning   Every year for up to five years, then every two.
Wiring   March.
Propagation   Seed or cuttings. Seed: sow in April in compost Code 1 at a temperature of 16°C (61°F). Cuttings: young and semi-ripe cuttings with a heel taken between the months of April and May in a compost Code 2 at a temperature between 16–18°C (61–64°F).
Pests   Mealybug.
Diseases   Mainly trouble-free.

Adansonia digitata (baobab)

The baobab is a very large, deciduous tree found in parts of Africa and famous for its trunk which is shaped like a bottle. The tree can live to a great age, but it is not a bonsai for the beginner.

Compost   Code 4.
Position   Plenty of light and good ventilation.

Temperature   Between 16–18°C (61–64°F).
Watering   Summer: every day; winter: every two to three days.
Root pruning   Every year for up to five years, then every two to three.
Wiring   Not required.
Propagation   Seed: sow in April in a compost Code 1, with a temperature of 21°C (70°F).
Pests   Red spider mite.
Diseases   Wilt and mildew. Allow air to flow freely around the bonsai.

Araucaria araucana (monkey puzzle)

This evergreen tree from Chile will make an excellent cold room bonsai and is ideal starting material for the beginner. There is a less hardy form, called the 'Norfolk Island pine' (*Araucaria heterophylla*), but it does not form such a good shape as the *Araucaria araucana*.

Compost   Code 4.
Position   Plenty of light and good ventilation; place in a frost-free room.
Temperature   Winter: between 5–10°C (41–50°F). Summer: between 16–18°C (61–64°F).
Watering   Summer: every day. Winter: every two to three days.

A two-year-old monkey puzzle (also known as elephant's foot).

Root pruning   Every year for up to five years, then every two.
Wiring   March–August.
Propagation   Seed: sow in March in compost Code 1, at a temperature of 13°C (55°F).
Pests   Mainly trouble-free.
Diseases   Mainly trouble-free.

Azalea

See Rhododendron

Bambusa multiplex (bamboo)

Habit   Good bamboo grass for indoor cultivation.
Compost   Code 3.
Position   Part-shade or sun.
Root pruning   Every year for up to five years, then every two.

[150]

Wiring   None.
Propagation   Division.
Pests   Mainly trouble-free.
Diseases   Mildew.

Bottle tree with an unusual root system. This tree originates from Australia.

Brachychiton ruspestris (bottle tree)

The bottle tree orginates from north-east Australia. It has a very thick and unusually-shaped trunk. The tree will tolerate very dry conditions and makes an excellent indoor bonsai for the beginner.

Compost   Code 3.
Position   Plenty of light; will even tolerate direct sunlight.
Temperature   Between 10–24°C (50–75°F).
Watering   Summer: check compost every three days, but as a general rule, water once a week. Winter: water once a fortnight, but continue to test the compost; never let it completely dry out.
Root pruning   Every three years.
Wiring   Not required.

> **Styles for the Bottle tree**
>
> *Chokkan*   Formal upright or straight-trunk style.
> *Moyogi*   Curving or informal upright trunk.
> *Shakan*   Leaning or slanting trunk.
> *Hokidachi*   Broom style, the head or foliage is shaped like a broom.
> *Neagari*   Exposed root system.
> *Ishitsuki*   Tree or trees grown on a rock.

Propagation   Mature trees can be purchased from your closest bonsai centre at a fairly low cost.
Pests   Red spider mite.
Diseases   Mainly trouble-free.

Carmona microphylla (carmona)

This evergreen tree bears white flowers followed by berries, reddish in colour. Very tree-like without too much training.

> **Styles for the Carmona**
>
> *Chokkan*   Formal upright or straight-trunk style.
> *Moyogi*   Curving or informal upright trunk.
> *Shakan*   Leaning or slanting trunk.
> *Bankan*   Twisted trunk, coiled almost like a spring.
> *So-kan*   Double trunk which divides close to the base of the trunk.
> *Kabudachi*   Multiple trunk – single tree at the base, splitting into several trunks to form a group.
> *Hokidachi*   Broom style, the head or foliage is shaped like a broom.
> *Fukinagashi*   Windswept style – all the branches lean in one direction.
> *Neagari*   Exposed root system.
> *Ishitsuki*   Tree or trees grown on a rock.
> *Yose-ue*   Group planting which resembles a forest.

Compost Code 4.
Position Plenty of light, but not direct sunlight.
Temperature Between 15–24°C (59–75°F).
Watering Summer: every day. Winter: every two to three days.
Root pruning Every year for up to five years, then every two.
Wiring March.
Propagation Seed and cuttings. Seed: sow in compost Code 1, at a temperature between 16–18°C (61–64°F). Cuttings: softwood or semi-ripe in compost Code 2, at a temperature of 18°C (64°F).
Pests Aphids, red spider mite.
Diseases Die-back and wilt.

Casuarina equisetifolia (beefwood tree)

Evergreen tree from Malaya with tufted needles. Fairly easy to grow. Another small *Casuarina* is the 'Dwarf Sheoke' variety, or *Casuarina nana*, a good tree for the beginner.

Styles for the Beefwood Tree

Chokkan Formal upright or straight-trunk style.
Moyogi Curving or informal upright trunk.
Shakan Leaning or slanting trunk.
Bankan Twisted trunk, coiled almost like a spring.
So-kan Double trunk which divides close to the base of the trunk.
Kabudachi Multiple trunk – single tree at the base, splitting into several trunks to form a group.
Hokidachi Broom style, the head or foliage is shaped like a broom.
Fukinagashi Windswept style – all the branches lean in one direction.
Neagari Exposed root system.
Netsuranari Connecting-root style – an odd number of trees growing from the same root system.
Ishitsuki Tree or trees grown on a rock.
Ikadabuki Raft style – the trunk leans on its side and the branches are only allowed to develop on one side, giving the illusion of several trees growing in a clump.

Compost Code 4.
Position Plenty of light, but not direct sunlight.
Temperature 16–18°C (61–64°F).
Watering Summer: every day; winter: every two to three days.
Root pruning Every year for up to five years, then every two.
Wiring March.
Propagation Seed: sow in compost Code 1, with a temperature of 16°C (61°F).
Pests Aphids, red spider mite.
Diseases Mainly trouble-free.

Styles for the Carob

Chokkan Formal upright or straight-trunk style.
Moyogi Curving or informal upright trunk.
Shakan Leaning or slanting trunk.
Bankan Twisted trunk, coiled almost like a spring.
So-kan Double trunk which divides close to the base of the trunk.
Kabudachi Multiple trunk – single tree at the base, splitting into several trunks to form a group.
Hokidachi Broom style, the head or foliage is shaped like a broom.
Fukinagashi Windswept style – all the branches lean in one direction.
Neagari Exposed root system.
Ishitsuki Tree or trees grown on a rock.

Ceratonia siliqua (carob) 'St John's Bread'

Evergreen tree, very easy to grow making it an ideal indoor bonsai for the beginner.

Compost Code 4.
Position Plenty of light.
Temperature Between 16–18°C (61–64°F).
Watering Summer: every day; winter: every two to three days.
Root pruning Every year for up to five years, then every two.
Wiring March.

Propagation   Seed: sow in compost Code 1, with a temperature of 16°C (61°F).
Pests   Mainly trouble-free.
Diseases   Mainly trouble-free.

Chamaedorea elegans (parlour palm)

Parlour palms are mainly used as a common houseplant and can be found in most garden centres or flower shops, hence its inclusion in this chapter as a cheap and widely available specimen.

Compost   Code 4.
Position   Plenty of light and good ventilation.
Temperature   All-year-round temperature between 10–22°C (50–72°F).
Watering   Summer: every day; winter: every day if grown over rock or in tufa. If grown in a pot, water every two to three days.
Root pruning   Every three years if grown in a pot: no root pruning if grown in tufa.
Wiring   Not required.
Propagation   It is less costly and time-consuming for the beginner to purchase a palm from a garden centre or florist's shop.

The palm tree is very easy to grow. Here, the root system is growing in the tufa.

Pests   Red spider mite.
Diseases   Mildew.

Styles for the Parlour Palm

Kabudachi   Multiple trunk – single tree at the base, splitting into several trunks to form a group.
Neagari   Exposed root system.
Ishitsuki   Tree or trees grown on a rock.

Citrus limon (lemon)

Small-growing tree from east Asia and less hardy than other *Citrus* bonsai. It bears fragrant flowers, followed by fruits. The fruit would be too large for a small bonsai, therefore grow as a large specimen tree. Grow in a constant warm temperature with plenty of light.

Styles for the Lemon

Chokkan   Formal upright or straight-trunk style.
Moyogi   Curving or informal upright trunk.
Shakan   Leaning or slanting trunk.
Bankan   Twisted trunk, coiled almost like a spring.
So-kan   Double trunk which divides close to the base of the trunk.
Kabudachi   Multiple trunk – single tree at the base, splitting into several trunks to form a group.
Hokidachi   Broom style, the head or foliage is shaped like a broom.
Fukinagashi   Windswept style – all the branches lean in one direction.
Neagari   Exposed root system.
Ishitsuki   Tree or trees grown on a rock.

Compost   Code 4.
Position   Full light, but not direct sunlight, good ventilation.
Temperature   Winter: 10°C (50°F). Summer: 18°C (64°F).

[153]

Watering Summer: every day; winter: every two to three days.

Root pruning The lemon tree does not like root pruning, therefore, prune every three years between the months of November and December. After pruning, do not overwater for the next two to four weeks and do not feed for four weeks.

Wiring March.

Propagation Seed or cuttings. Seed: sow in March in a compost Code 1 at a temperature of 16°C (61°F). Cuttings: semi-ripe cuttings taken in the last two weeks of July or the first two in August. Place them in a compost Code 2 with bottom heat at a temperature of 18°C (64°F).

Pests Mealybug.

Diseases Mainly trouble-free.

Citrus medica (citron)

Small tree from the Far East; makes an excellent

Styles for the Citron

Chokkan Formal upright or straight-trunk style.
Moyogi Curving or informal upright trunk.
Shakan Leaning or slanting trunk.
Bankan Twisted trunk, coiled almost like a spring.
So-kan Double trunk which divides close to the base of the trunk.
Kabudachi Multiple trunk at the base, splitting into several trunks to form a group.
Hokidachi Broom style, the head or foliage is shaped like a broom.
Fukinagashi Windswept style – all the branches lean in one direction.
Neagari Exposed root system.
Netsuranari Connecting-root style – an odd number of trees growing from the same root system.
Ishitsuki Tree or trees grown on a rock.
Ikadabuki Raft style – the trunk leans on its side and the branches are only allowed to develop on one side, giving the impression of several trees growing in a clump.
Yose-ue Group planting which resembles a forest.

semi-cold-room bonsai. The flowers are pinkish-white and fragrant, although the fruits are too heavy for the tree. Remove the flowers once they have gone over or just before they set seed.

Compost Code 4.

Position Plenty of light.

Temperature Between 18–21°C (64–70°F), never allow winter temperatures to fall below 13°C (55°F).

Watering Summer: every day; winter: every two to three days.

Root pruning Every two years for up to six years, then every three.

Wiring March.

Propagation Seed or cuttings. Seed: sow in compost Code 1, at a temperature of 16°C (61°F). Cuttings: semi-ripe, with bottom heat at a temperature of 18°C (64°F).

Pests Red spider mite.

Diseases Mainly trouble-free.

Citrus mitis (orange)

This tree from the Philippines will make an excellent flowering indoor bonsai and, if grown as a large specimen, it will also make a good fruiting bonsai. The flowers are white and very fragrant, which adds to the beauty of the tree.

Compost Code 4.

Position Plenty of light and sun, but shade on very hot, sunny days. Good ventilation and a frost-free room.

Temperature Winter: never allow to drop below 13°C (55°F). Summer: keep between 18–21°C (64–70°F).

Watering Summer: every day; winter: every two to three days.

Root pruning Every two years for up to four, then every three.

Wiring March.

Propagation Seed or cuttings. Seed: sow in March in composet Code 1, at a temperature of 16°C (61°F). Cuttings: take semi-ripe cuttings between the months of July and August. Place in compost Code 2 with a bottom heat temperature of 18°C (64°F).

Pests Mealy bug.

Diseases Mainly trouble-free.

Styles for the Orange Tree

Chokkan Formal upright or straight-trunk style.
Moyogi Curving or informal upright trunk.
Shakan Leaning or slanting trunk.
Bankan Twisted trunk, coiled almost like a spring.
So-kan Double trunk which divides close to the base of the trunk.
Kabudachi Multiple trunk – single tree at the base, splitting into several trunks to form a group.
Hokidachi Broom style, the head or foliage is shaped like a broom.
Neagari Exposed root system.
Ishitsuki Tree or trees grown on a rock.

months, full light during the winter. Keep the compost moist throughout the summer.
Temperature Winter: between 7–10°C (45–50°F); summer: 18°C (64°F).
Watering Summer: every day; winter: every two to three days.

Styles for the Grapefruit

Chokkan Formal upright or straight-trunk style.
Moyogi Curving or informal upright trunk.
Shakan Leaning or slanting trunk.
Bankan Twisted trunk, coiled almost like a spring.
So-kan Double trunk which divides close to the base of the trunk.
Kabudachi Multiple trunk – single tree at the base, splitting into several trunks to form a group.
Hokidachi Broom style, the head or foliage is shaped like a broom.
Fukinagashi Windswept style – all the branches lean in one direction.
Neagari Exposed root system.
Ishitsuki Tree or trees grown on a rock.

Citrus paradisi (grapefruit)

Semi-cold-room indoor bonsai. The flowers are white and the fruits far too large for bonsai; re-move flowers before they set seed.

Compost Code 4.
Position Part-shade during the summer

Grapefruit and grapefruit in flower. This is grown from seed or available from garden centres as a seedling. You will have to sacrifice the fruit if you want to concentrate on the shape, and sacrifice shape if you want the bonsai to produce fruit.

[155]

Root pruning Grapefruit do not like root pruning, therefore, prune every three years in October–November.
Wiring March.
Propagation Seed and cuttings. Seed: sow in March in compost Code 1, at a temperature of 16°C (61°F). Cuttings: take semi-ripe cuttings 7.5–10cm (3–4in) during the months of July and August, in compost Code 2 with a bottom heat temperature of 18°C (64°F).
Pests Mealybug.
Diseases Mainly trouble-free.

Crassula, many forms (jade tree)

Classed as a houseplant, although the Japanese and Chinese have been using it for many years as a bonsai. Also called the 'money tree', it is easy to look after and makes an excellent tree for the beginner. However, the jade tree can become top-heavy if left unpruned.

Compost Code 4.
Position Good light and plenty of sun.
Temperature Winter: should not fall below

Styles for the Jade Tree

Chokkan Formal upright or straight-trunk style.
So-kan Double trunk which divides close to the base of the trunk.
Kabudachi Multiple trunk – single tree at the base, splitting into several trunks to form a group.
Hokidachi Broom style, the head or foliage is shaped like a broom.
Fukinagashi Windswept style – all the branches lean in one direction.
Neagari Exposed root system.
Netsuranari Connecting-root style – an odd number of trees growing from the same root system.
Ishitsuki Tree or trees grown on a rock.
Ikadabuki Raft style – the trunk leans on its side and the branches are only allowed to develop on one side, giving the impression of several trees growing in a clump.

10°C (50°F), although it will tolerate slightly lower temperatures. Summer: between 16–18°C (61–64°F).
Watering Summer: every one to two days; every three to four days during the winter.
Root pruning Every three years. (Keep pinching back top growth.)
Wiring March.
Propagation Very easy from leaf cuttings. During the spring, remove a leaf and allow it to dry for a day or two, then pin to the surface of compost Code 2.
Pests Mealybug.
Diseases Mainly trouble-free.

Cycas revoluta (sago palm)

Grown as an artistic bonsai and could easily be confused for a glorified houseplant. As a bonsai, the sago expresses itself best when grown over or planted into volcanic rock. Display the sago in a deep pot, similar to the type used for cascade plantings. The pot should have artistic Japanese or Chinese markings on it.

Styles for the Sago Palm

Kabudachi Multiple trunk – single tree at the base, splitting into several trunks to form a group.
Neagari Exposed root system.
Ishitsuki Tree or trees grown on a rock.

Compost Code 4.
Position Sun or part-shade.
Temperature Winter: should never fall below 10°C (50°F). Summer: between 16–18°C (61–64°F).
Watering Summer: every day; for those bonsai planted in volcanic rock or tufa, you may need to water twice a day.
Root pruning Every three years, may be troublesome. When grown in a rock no root pruning is required.
Wiring Not required.
Propagation Seed: sow between February and April in compost Code 1 with a temperature of 24°C (75°F). Due to the size of the seed, use a

deep seed tray or pot. Remove suckers during April and May and place into compost Code 4.
Pests   Red spider mite.
Diseases   Mainly trouble-free.

Dracaena draco (dragon tree)

Evergreen indoor bonsai from the Canary Islands. This is an excellent tree for the beginner or the person who cannot spend too much time on their tree. One such tree (found on one of the Canary Islands) is said to be up to 1,000 years old.

Compost   Code 4.
Position   Plenty of light and good ventilation.
Temperature   Winter: 10°C (50°F), but will tolerate slightly lower temperatures. Summer: between 16–18°C (61–64°F).
Watering   Summer: every day; winter: every two to three days.
Root pruning   Carefully prune the root every two years. Do not overwater for the next three weeks and stop feeding for one month.
Wiring   Not required.
Propagation   Cuttings: most good garden

The dragon tree is commonly available and an easy bonsai to create. Variegated foliage adds variety to this well-known houseplant.

Styles for the Dragon Tree

Chokkan   Formal upright or straight-trunk style.
Moyogi   Curving or informal upright trunk.
Shakan   Leaning or slanting trunk.
Bankan   Twisted trunk, coiled almost like a spring.
So-kan   Double trunk which divides close to the base of the trunk.
Neagari   Exposed root system.
Ishitsuki   Tree or trees grown on a rock.

---

centres with a houseplant section should be able to supply you with your first seedling or plant. From this 7.5cm (3in) mature stem, cuttings can be taken in April and placed in a compost Code 2 on a warm bench or in a propagator at a temperature of 21°C (70°F).
Pests   Root mealybug and red spider mite.
Diseases   Mainly trouble-free.

Erythrina indica (coral tree)

A deciduous, flowering, cold-room bonsai tree from India, also known as 'crab claw' and 'tiger's claw'. The tree owes its common name to its claw-shaped flowers. The flowers are crimson and are followed by attractive pods.

Compost   Code 3.
Position   Light shade through the summer months.
Temperature   Winter: never allow to drop below 7°C (45°F). Summer: place in a cool room with a temperature of 16°C (61°F).
Watering   Summer: every day; winter: every two to three days.
Root pruning   Every year for up to five years, then every two or three, depending on the rate of growth.
Wiring   March and August.
Propagation   Seed or cuttings. Seed: sow in compost Code 1 at a temperature of 16°C (61°F). Cuttings: taken with a heel.
Pests   Red spider mite.
Diseases   Mainly trouble-free.

Styles for the Coral Tree

Chokkan   Formal upright or straight-trunk style.
Moyogi   Curving or informal upright trunk.
Shakan   Leaning or slanting trunk.
Bankan   Twisted trunk, coiled almost like a spring.
So-kan   Double trunk which divides close to the base of the trunk.
Kabudachi   Multiple trunk – single tree at the base, splitting into several trunks to form a group.
Hokidachi   Broom style, the head or foliage is shaped like a broom.
Fukinagashi   Windswept style – all the branches lean in one direction.
Neagari   Exposed root system.
Netsuranari   Connecting-root style – an odd number of trees growing from the same root system.
Ishitsuki   Tree or trees grown on a rock.
Ikadabuki   Raft style – the trunk leans on its side and the branches are only allowed to develop on one side, giving the illusion of several trees growing in a clump.
Yose-ue   Group planting which resembles a forest.

Styles for the Lemon Tree

Chokkan   Formal upright or straight-trunk style.
Moyogi   Curving or informal upright trunk.
Shakan   Leaning or slanting trunk.
Bankan   Twisted trunk, coiled almost like a spring.
So-kan   Double trunk which divides close to the base of the trunk.
Kabudachi   Multiple trunk – single tree at the base, splitting into several trunks to form a group.
Hokidachi   Broom style, the head or foliage is shaped like a broom.
Fukinagashi   Windswept style – all the branches lean in one direction.
Neagari   Exposed root system.
Ishitsuki   Tree or trees grown on a rock.

Eucalyptus globulus (blue gum)

A tender, colourful evergreen tree from Tasmania, used in some gardens as a bedding plant during the summer months and available from

Eucalyptus citriodora (lemon)

Compost   Code 4; keep moist during the summer months.
Position   Plenty of light, place outside on warm days.
Temperature   Cold room with a temperature of 10°C (50°F).
Watering   Summer: every day; winter: every two to three days.
Root pruning   Every two years for up to five years, then every three. Take extra care when root pruning because roots are prone to rotting.
Wiring   March.
Propagation   Seed: sow between February and March in compost Code 1, with a temperature between 13–16°C (55–61°F).
Pests   Red spider mite and mealybug.
Diseases   Mainly trouble-free.

Blue gum originates from Australia. It is best kept in a cold room indoors.

[158]

local nurseries. It has blue-white smooth bark, white flowers and large black fruits.

Compost   Code 4; keep compost moist during the summer months.
Position   Plenty of light and full sun; place outside on warm days during the summer.
Temperature   Cold room with a temperature of about 16°C (61°F).
Watering   Summer: every day; winter: every two to three days.
Root pruning   Carefully root-prune every two to four years then every three. May be troublesome.
Wiring   March.
Propagation   Seed: sow between February and March in compost Code 1, with a temperature of 13–16°C (55–61°F). Cover seed tray with a propagator top.
Pests   Mainly trouble-free.
Diseases   Mainly trouble-free.

Styles for the Blue Gum

Chokkan   Formal upright or straight-trunk style.
Moyogi   Curving or informal upright trunk.
Shakan   Leaning or slanting trunk.
Bankan   Twisted trunk, coiled almost like a spring.
So-kan   Double trunk which divides close to the base of the trunk.
Kabudachi   Multiple trunk – single tree at the base, splitting into several trunks to form a group.
Hokidachi   Broom style, the head or foliage is shaped like a broom.
Fukinagashi   Windswept style – all the branches lean in one direction.
Neagari   Exposed root system.
Netsuranari   Connecting-root style – an odd number of trees growing from the same root system.
Ishitsuki   Tree or trees grown on a rock.
Ikadabuki   Raft style – the trunk leans on its side and the branches are only allowed to develop on one side, giving the illusion of several trees growing in a clump.
Yose-ue   Group planting which resembles a forest.

Eucalyptus gunnii (cider gum)

Originating from southern areas of Australia, this evergreen cold-room bonsai is placed outside during the summer months. It has a very attractive smooth and grey bark and bears white fluffy flowers which form in clusters of three, followed by white, flat-ended capsules.

Styles for the Cider Gum

Chokkan   Formal upright or straight-trunk style.
Moyogi   Curving or informal upright trunk.
Shakan   Leaning or slanting trunk.
Bankan   Twisted trunk, coiled almost like a spring.
So-kan   Double trunk which divides close to the base of the trunk.
Kabudachi   Multiple trunk – single tree at the base, splitting into several trunks to form a group.
Hokidachi   Broom style, the head or foliage is shaped like a broom.
Fukinagashi   Windswept style – all the branches lean in one direction.
Neagari   Exposed root system.
Netsuranari   Connecting-root style – an odd number of trees growing from the same root system.
Ishitsuki   Tree or trees grown on a rock.
Ikadabuki   Raft style – the trunk leans on its side and the branches are only allowed to develop on one side, giving the illusion of several trees growing in a clump.
Yose-ue   Group planting which resembles a forest.

Compost   Code 4; keep compost moist during the summer months.
Position   Plenty of light, place outside on warm days.
Temperature   Cold room, with a temperature of 16°C (61°F).
Watering   Summer: every day; winter: every two to three days.
Root pruning   Prune every two years for up to four years, then every three. Take care when root pruning; roots are prone to rotting.
Wiring   March.

Propagation Seed: sow between February and March in compost Code 1, with a temperature of 13–16°C (55–61°F). Cover seed tray with a propagator lid or a piece of glass.
Pests Mainly trouble-free.
Diseases Mainly trouble-free.

Ficus deltoidea, F. diversifolia (fig)

Evergreen tree from India, also known as the mistletoe fig or cherry banyan, which produces yellow-red fruits. A good fruiting bonsai for the beginner.

Compost Code 4.
Position Plenty of light, but not direct sunlight, and good ventilation.
Temperature Winter: 10°C (50°F). Summer 16–18°C (61–64°F).

Styles for the Fig

Chokkan Formal upright or straight-trunk style.
Moyogi Curving or informal upright trunk.
Shakan Leaning or slanting trunk.
Bankan Twisted trunk, coiled almost like a spring.
So-kan Double trunk which divides close to the base of the trunk.
Kabudachi Multiple trunk – single tree at the base, splitting into several trunks to form a group.
Hokidachi Broom style, the head or foliage is shaped like a broom.
Fukinagashi Windswept style – all the branches lean in one direction.
Neagari Exposed root system.
Netsuranari Connecting-root style – an odd number of trees growing from the same root system.
Ishitsuki Tree or trees grown on a rock.
Ikadabuki Raft style – the trunk leans on its side and the branches are only allowed to develop on one side, giving the illusion of several trees growing in a clump.
Yose-ue Group planting which resembles a forest.

Watering Summer: every day; winter: every two to three days.
Root pruning Every two years. May be troublesome.
Wiring March.
Propagation Plant should be available from good garden centres with houseplant sections, or obtained from cuttings and air-layering. Cuttings: can be taken between the months of April and June. Take side shoots between 7.5–10cm (3–4in) long and place them in compost Code 2 with a temperature of 18°C (64°F).
Pests Scale insects.
Diseases Root rot (*see* Chapter 5).

Gardenia jasminoides (gardenia)

Small shrub-like tree. An excellent flowering bonsai, very scented, but not a tree for the beginner.

Compost Code 4.
Position Plenty of light during the winter, part-shade in the summer with good ventilation.
Temperature Winter: between 12–16°C (54–61°F). Summer: between 16–18°C (61–64°F).

The gardenia is more of a cold-room bonsai. It is difficult to grow but will bear fragrant white blooms after a good ten years.

[160]

Styles for the Gardenia

Chokkan   Formal upright or straight-trunk style.
Moyogi   Curving or informal upright trunk.
Shakan   Leaning or slanting trunk.
Bankan   Twisted trunk, coiled almost like a spring.
So-kan   Double trunk which divides close to the base of the trunk.
Kabudachi   Multiple trunk – single tree at the base, splitting into several trunks to form a group.
Hokidachi   Broom style, the head or foliage is shaped like a broom.
Fukinagashi   Windswept style – all the branches lean in one direction.
Neagari   Exposed root system.
Netsuranari   Connecting-root style – an odd number of trees growing from the same root system.
Ishitsuki   Tree or trees grown on a rock.
Ikadabuki   Raft style – the trunk leans on its side and the branches are only allowed to develop on one side, giving the illusion of several trees growing in a clump.
Yose-ue   Group planting which resembles a forest.

Watering   Summer: every day; keep the atmosphere humid during warm, sunny days by using a humidity tray or mist spray gun. (Do not mist in direct sunlight.) Winter: water every two to three days.
Root pruning   Every two years.
Wiring   March.
Propagation   The first plant can be purchased from a good garden centre with a houseplant section and then cuttings. Cuttings: non-flowering side shoots taken with a heel during the months of February to March in a compost Code 2 at a temperature of 18–21°C (64–70°F).
Pests   Aphids and red spider mite.
Diseases   Bud drop.

Lagerstroemia indica (Chinese crape myrtle)

Habit   Deciduous bonsai with pink, white or lilac flowers.

Compost   Code 3.
Position   Part-shade or sun.
Root pruning   Every year for up to five years, then every two.
Wiring   During the growing season, except when flowering.
Propagation   Seed or cutting.
Pests   Aphids, red spider mite.
Diseases   Mildew.

Malpighia glabra, M. coccigera (Barbados cherry)

Evergreen tree from the West Indies, produces pink flowers.

Compost   Code 4.
Position   Plenty of light but not direct sunlight.
Temperature   Should not drop below 18°C (64°F) and never rise above 24°C (75°F).
Watering   Summer: every day; winter: every two to three days.
Root pruning   Every year up to five years, then every two.
Wiring   March.
Propagation   Seed and cuttings. Seed, sow in April in a compost Code 1, with a temperature of 21°C (70°F). Cuttings: April, softwood cuttings in compost Code 2, bottom heat between 21–25°C (70–77°F).

Styles for the Barbados Cherry

Chokkan   Formal upright or straight-trunk style.
Moyogi   Curving or informal upright trunk.
Shakan   Leaning or slanting trunk.
Bankan   Twisted trunk, coiled almost like a spring.
So-kan   Double trunk which divides close to the base of the trunk.
Hokidachi   Broom style, the head or foliage is shaped like a broom.
Fukinagashi   Windswept style – all the branches lean in one direction.
Neagari   Exposed root system.
Ishitsuki   Tree or trees grown on a rock.

Pests Aphids, red spider mite.
Diseases Mainly trouble-free, but prune to allow light and air into the centre of the tree.

Metrosideros tomentosa (Christmas torch)

Evergreen tree from New Zealand and an excellent bonsai. Also called the Christmas Tree, it produces flowers which resemble candles.

Compost Code 4.
Position Plenty of light, but not direct sunlight.
Temperature Between 16–18°C (61–64°F).
Watering Summer: every day; winter: every two to three days.

Styles for the Christmas Torch

Chokkan Formal upright or straight-trunk style.
Moyogi Curving or informal upright trunk.
Shakan Leaning or slanting trunk.
Bankan Twisted trunk, coiled almost like a spring.
So-kan Double trunk which divides close to the base of the trunk.
Kabudachi Multiple trunk – single tree at the base, splitting into several trunks to form a group.
Hokidachi Broom style, the head or foliage is shaped like a broom.
Fukinagashi Windswept style – all the branches lean in one direction.
Neagari Exposed root system.
Ishitsuki Tree or trees grown on a rock.

Root pruning Every year for up to five years, then every two.
Wiring March.
Propagation Seed: sow in compost Code 4, at a temperature of 18°C (64°F).
Pests Mainly trouble-free.
Diseases Mainly trouble-free.

Murraya paniculata (jasmine orange)

Habit Evergreen bonsai with strong scented flowers followed by red berries.
Compost Code 3.
Position Part-shade or sun.
Root pruning Every year for up to five years, then every two.
Wiring During the growing season.
Pests Aphids, red spider mite.
Diseases Mildew, die-back.

Styles for the Banana Tree

Chokkan Formal upright or straight-trunk style.
Shakan Leaning or slanting trunk.
Neagari Exposed root system.
Ishitsuki Tree or trees grown on a rock.

Musa taiwan (banana)

Deciduous dwarf banana tree from China. To produce the fruit for showing you would need to grow a large specimen bonsai, therefore, this is not a tree for the beginner. A small form from the Canary Islands is *Musa cavendisbii/Musa acuminata* or 'Dwarf Cavendish'.

Compost Code 4.
Position Light shade from May to August; during winter, full light.
Temperature Winter: never allow to drop below 10°C (50°F). Summer: try to keep the temperature below 21°C (70°F).

Styles for the Banana Tree

Chokkan Formal upright or straight-trunk style.
Shakan Leaning or slanting trunk.
Neagari Exposed root system.
Ishitsuki Tree or trees grown on a rock.

Watering Summer; every day; winter: every two to three days.
Root pruning Every two to three years, with great care. May be troublesome.
Wiring March.
Propagation Seed: sow in April in a compost Code 1, with a temperature of 21°C (70°F).
Pests Red spider mite.
Diseases Mildew; allow for ventilation.

One of the myrtle's best features is its fragrant foliage.

Myrtus communis (myrtle)

Evergreen tree from Greece, good cold-room flowering bonsai with aromatic leaves. Flowers from June and can last until August. White flowers followed by purple-to-black fruits.

Compost Code 4.
Position Plenty of light and part-sun, good ventilation; keep compost moist during the summer months.
Temperature Winter: between 5–10°C (45–50°F). Summer: between 16–18°C (61–64°F).
Watering Summer; every day; winter: every two to three days.
Root pruning Every year for up to five years, then every two.
Wiring March.

Styles for the Myrtle

Chokkan Formal upright or straight-trunk style.
Moyogi Curving or informal upright trunk.
Shakan Leaning or slanting trunk.
Bankan Twisted trunk, coiled almost like a spring.
So-kan Double trunk which divides close to the base of the trunk.
Kabudachi Multiple trunk – single tree at the base, splitting into several trunks to form a group.
Hokidachi Broom style, the head or foliage is shaped like a broom.
Fukinagashi Windswept style – all the branches lean in one direction.
Neagari Exposed root system.
Yose-ue Group planting which resembles a forest.
Ishitsuki Tree or trees grown on a rock.

Propagation Purchase first plant from the houseplant section of a good garden centre or bonsai nursery and use it as a stock plant to take cuttings. Cuttings: take non-flowering side shoots between 5–7.5cm (3–4in) in length with a heel. Use compost Code 2 and a bottom heat temperature of 16°C (61°F).
Pests Mainly trouble-free.
Diseases Mainly trouble-free.

Nandina domestica (Chinese sacred bamboo)

Small shrub from China which will, given time, form into a cold-room flowering bonsai. The flowers are white during the month of July, followed by a white fruit in August. This is really a semi-indoor bonsai and therfore will need a rest period during the winter. Good autumn colour just before the bonsai drops some of its old foliage.

Compost Code 4.
Position Cool room, but frost-free. Plenty of light during winter and summer and good ventilation.
Temperature Winter 10°C (50°F), but will

Styles for the Chinese Sacred Bamboo

Chokkan   Formal upright or straight-trunk style.
Kabudachi   Multiple trunk – single tree at the base, splitting into several trunks to form a group.
Fukinagashi   Windswept style – all the branches lean in one direction.
Neagari   Exposed root system.
Netsuranari   Connecting-root style – an odd number of trees growing from the same root system.
Ishitsuki   Tree or trees grown on a rock.
Ikadabuki   Raft style – the trunk leans on its side and the branches are only allowed to develop on one side, giving the illusion of several trees growing in a clump.
Yose-ue   Group planting which resembles a forest.

tolerate lower temperatures. Summer: between 16–18°C (61–64°F).
Watering   Summer: every day; winter: twice a week.
Root pruning   Every year for up to five years, then every two.
Wiring   Not required.
Propagation   Seed and cuttings. Seed: sow in seed trays and place outside to overwinter in compost Code 1, without temperature. Cuttings: treat in the same way as a hardwood cutting, but place in a pot or tray and then in a coldframe or glasshouse.
Pests   Mainly trouble-free.
Diseases   Mainly trouble-free, but prune to allow light and air into the centre of the tree.

Olea (olive tree)

Evergreen cold-room bonsai, but will take several years before it starts to bear fruits.

Compost   Code 4.
Position   Plenty of light but not direct sunlight.
Temperature   Winter: temperatures should remain at 10°C (50°F), but the bonsai will tolerate slightly lower temperature for very short

Young sacred bamboo planted with driftwood. Suitable for cold room.

Styles for the Olive Tree

Chokkan   Formal upright or straight-trunk style.
Moyogi   Curving or informal upright trunk.
Shakan   Leaning or slanting trunk.
Bankan   Twisted trunk, coiled almost like a spring.
So-kan   Double trunk which divides close to the base of the trunk.
Kabudachi   Multiple trunk – single tree at the base, splitting into several trunks to form a group.
Hokidachi   Broom style, the head or foliage is shaped like a broom.
Fukinagashi   Windswept style – all the branches lean in one direction.
Neagari   Exposed root system.
Ishitsuki   Tree or trees grown on a rock.
Yose-ue   Group planting which resembles a forest.

periods. Summer: between 16–18°C (61–64°F); these temperatures should be maintained as far as possible.

Watering   Summer: every day; winter: every two to three days.

Root pruning   Every year for up to five years, then every two.

Wiring   March.

Propagation   Cuttings: take semi-ripe cuttings in July and place in a coldframe or glasshouse. Use compost Code 2 and bottom heat with a temperature between 16–18°C (61–64°F).

Pests   Mainly trouble-free.

Diseases   Mainly trouble-free.

Styles for the Malayan Apple

Chokkan   Formal upright or straight-trunk style.

Moyogi   Curving or informal upright trunk.

Shakan   Leaning or slanting trunk.

Bankan   Twisted trunk, coiled almost like a spring.

So-kan   Double trunk which divides close to the base of the trunk.

Kabudachi   Multiple trunk – single tree at the base, splitting into several trunks to form a group.

Hokidachi   Broom style, the head or foliage is shaped like a broom.

Fukinagashi   Windswept style – all the branches lean in one direction.

Neagari   Exposed root system.

Netsuranari   Connecting-root style – an odd number of trees growing from the same root system.

Ishitsuki   Tree or trees grown on a rock.

Ikadabuki   Raft style – the tree leans on its side and the branches are only allowed to develop on one side, giving the illusion of several trees growing in a clump.

Yose-ue   Group planting which resembles a forest.

Patanga (Malayan apple)

Interesting flowering cold room bonsai, with white 'fluffy' flowers. The fruit is small and red-to-purple in colour, resembling a crab apple fruit.

The Malayan apple, here showing fruit. It makes an ideal beginner's plant.

Compost   Code 4.

Position   Full light, but not direct sunlight, good ventilation.

Temperature   Winter: do not allow to drop below 10°C (50°F). Summer: between 16–21°C (61–70°F).

Watering   Summer: every two to three days; winter: once or twice a week.

Root pruning   Every year for up to five years, then every two.

Wiring   March.

Propagation   Seed or cuttings.

Pests   Mainly trouble-free.

Diseases   Mainly trouble-free.

Phoenix roebelenii (date palm)

Evergreen palm from Asia, excellent indoor bonsai, especially when grown in volcanic rock.

Compost   Code 3 or volcanic rock and tufa.

Position   Light shade and good ventilation. Keep the compost between dry and moist during the winter months.

Temperature   Winter: never allow to drop below 13°C (55°F). Summer: 18°C (64°F).

Styles for the Date Palm

Kabudachi Multiple trunk – single tree at the base, splitting into several trunks to form a group.
Neagari Exposed root system.
Netsuranari Connecting-root style – an odd number of trees growing from the same root system.
Ishitsuki Tree or trees grown on a rock.

Watering Summer: the palm will need plenty of water plus misting with a hand spray. For those trees grown in the soft forms of volcanic or tufa rock, you may find the need to water twice a day. Winter: water every two to three days and mist to help control red spider.
Root pruning Every two years for pot-grown bonsai, no root pruning when grown in rock or tufa.
Wiring Not required.
Propagation Seed and suckers. Seed: sow between February and March in a compost Code 1 with a temperature between 18–21°C (64–70°F). Suckers: suckers can be transplanted during the month of May into individual

training pots with compost Code 3 and kept at a temperature between 18–21°C (64–70°F). Removing suckers is also a form of pruning, therefore, no other pruning is required.
Pests Mealybugs and red spider mite.
Diseases Mainly trouble-free.

See also Chamaedorea elegans (parlour palm).

Pinus halefecis (Jerusalem pine)

Cold room conditions should be given at all times. Although this pine will make an excellent bonsai, it may be troublesome until such time as you can find a balanced position – one that offers a low temperature without frost as well as good ventilation.

Compost Code 4.
Position Plenty of light in a cool room with good ventilation, away from radiators and warm-air ducts.

Styles for the Jerusalem Pine

Chokkan Formal upright or straight-trunk style.
Moyogi Curving or informal upright trunk.
Shakan Leaning or slanting trunk.
Bankan Twisted trunk, coiled almost like a spring.
So-kan Double trunk which divides close to the base of the trunk.
Kabudachi Multiple trunk – single tree at the base, splitting into several trunks to form a group.
Fukinagashi Windswept style – all the branches lean in one direction.
Neagari Exposed root system.
Netsuranari Connecting-root style – an odd number of trees growing from the same root system.
Ishitsuki Tree or trees grown on a rock.
Ikadabuki Raft style – the trunk leans on its side and the branches are only allowed to develop on one side, giving the illusion of several trees growing in a clump.
Yose-ue Group planting which resembles a forest.

Jerusalem pine. It is preferable to keep this tree in a cold room.

[166]

Temperature 10–18°C (50–64°F) throughout the year.
Watering Summer: every day; winter: every two to three days.
Root pruning Every year for up to five years, then every two or three, depending on the rate of growth.
Wiring March.
Propagation Seed or cuttings.
Pests Red spider mite.
Diseases Mildew.

Pistacia (pistachio)

Evergreen cold-room indoor bonsai with pinnate leaves and red fruits which are formed during the autumn.

Compost Code 4.
Postion A cool room with plenty of ventilation and light.
Temperature Summer: between 10–18°C (50–64°F). Winter: do not allow to drop below 10°C (50°F).

Styles for the Pistachio Tree

Chokkan Formal upright or straight-trunk style.
Moyogi Curving or informal upright trunk.
Shakan Leaning or slanting trunk.
Bankan Twisted trunk, coiled almost like a spring.
So-kan Double trunk which divides close to the base of the trunk.
Kabudachi Multiple trunk – single tree at the base, splitting into several trunks to form a group.
Hokidachi Broom style, the head is shaped like a broom.
Fukinagashi Windswept style – all the branches lean in one direction.
Neagari Exposed root system.
Netsuranari Connecting-root style – an odd number of trees growing from the same root system.
Ishitsuki Tree or trees grown on a rock.

Watering Every day during a warm summer; winter: every two to three days.
Root pruning Every year for up to five years, then every two or three depending on the rate of growth.
Wiring March.
Propagation Seed or cuttings.
Pests Mainly trouble free.
Diseases Mainly trouble free.

Punica granatum (pomegranate)

Small deciduous tree from Iran and suitable for either a cold or warm room. The flowers on the pomegranate are scarlet in colour and tubular in shape, flowering in the months between June and September.

Punica granatum 'Nana'

Smaller in size, flower and fruit than the *Punica granatum*, and more suitable to grow as a bonsai.

Autumn Pomegranates are deciduous trees and will therefore need a rest period during the winter months. However, first-time buyers and beginners to the art of bonsai should treat the tree

Pomegranate is one of the easiest trees to grow in a group, as shown here.

The fruits of the pomegranate will become too large and heavy for the fine branches.

as an evergreen. I have found that the pomegranate will tolerate indoor conditions, but only for a two-year period, after which it will need to be placed into a cold room and forced into dormancy for the winter period. Symptoms shown by the tree during the autumn and parts of the winter are as follows:

1. The tree may drop some or all of its leaves and then shoot new ones.
2. Leaves tend to look sick and dull.
3. The tree starts to flower.

Therefore, during the autumn and winter, the tree will need a constant level of light, a controlled temperature, ventilation and regular water. All these factors will help the photosynthesis process and produce sugar and starch. A feeding programme of a balanced fertilizer every month alternating with a tomato feed will help the tree through the winter period.

Compost Code 4.
Position Plenty of light and full sun, good ventilation at all times.
Temperature Winter: temperature can drop to 7°C (45°F) to allow the tree to drop its foliage. Summer: between 18–21°C (64–70°F). During dormancy keep the tree at a temperature of 7°C (45°F) from October through to March. Keep in totally frost-free conditions.
Watering Summer: every day; winter: every two to three days.

Styles for the Pomegranate

Chokkan Formal upright or straight-trunk style.
Moyogi Curving or informal upright trunk.
Shakan Leaning or slanting trunk.
Bankan Twisted trunk, coiled almost like a spring.
So-kan Double trunk which divides close to the base of the trunk.
Kabudachi Multiple trunk – single tree at the base, splitting into several trunks to form a group.
Hokidachi Broom style, the head or foliage is shaped like a broom.
Fukinagashi Windswept style – all the branches lean in one direction.
Neagari Exposed root system.
Netsuranari Connecting-root style – an odd number of trees growing from the same root system.
Ishitsuki Tree or trees grown on a rock.
Ikadabuki Raft style – the trunk leans on its side and the branches are only allowed to develop on one side, giving the illusion of several trees growing in a clump.
Yose-ue Group planting which resembles a forest.

Pomegranate in a boat-shaped pot.

[168]

Root pruning Every year for up for five years, then every two.
Wiring March and August.
Propagation Seed and cuttings. Seed: sow in March in a compost Code 1, with a temperature between 16–18°C (61–64°F). Cuttings: take semi-ripe cuttings with a heel, between 7.5–9cm (3–3.5in) long, during the latter part of July to the beginning of August. Place in a compost Code 2, with a bottom heat temperature of 16–18°C (61–64°F).
Pests Mainly trouble-free.
Diseases Mainly trouble-free.

Sageretia theezans (sageretia)

Evergreen tree from southern China with an interesting bark that flakes. The trunk will thicken in time.

Compost Code 4.
Position As much light as possible, misting is very beneficial.
Temperature Between 12–24°C (54–75°F).
Watering Summer: every day; winter: every two to three days.
Root pruning Every year for up to five years, then every two.

Styles for the Sageretia

Chokkan Formal upright or straight-trunk style.
Moyogi Curving or informal upright trunk.
Shakan Leaning or slanting trunk.
Bankan Twisted trunk, coiled almost like a spring.
So-kan Double trunk which divides close to the base of the trunk.
Kabudachi Multiple trunk – single tree at the base, splitting into several trunks to form a group.
Hokidachi Broom style, the head or foliage is shaped like a broom.
Fukinagashi Windswept style – all the branches lean in one direction.
Neagari Exposed root system.
Ishitsuki Tree or trees grown on a rock.

Wiring March.
Propagation Cuttings – soft and semi-ripe.
Pests Mainly trouble-free.
Diseases Mainly trouble-free.

Variegated serissa in flower. This type of serissa is easier to keep than the non-variegated one.

Serissa foetida (serissa or tree of a thousand stars)

Small tree from southern China and south-east Asia with a whitish trunk and white flowers which, as its name indicates, look like stars.

Compost Code 4.
Position As much light as possible but not direct sunlight. Try to minimize moving the tree from one position to another.
Temperature Keep the temperature between 10–18°C (50–60°F).
Watering Summer: every day and sometimes twice a day; do not over-water, but keep the compost moist. Winter: every one to two days depending on the temperature.

[169]

Serissa, or tree of a thousand stars whose white bark is particularly attractive.

Styles for the Serissa

Chokkan   Formal upright or straight-trunk style.
Moyogi   Curving or informal upright trunk.
Shakan   Leaning or slanting trunk.
Bankan   Twisted trunk, coiled almost like a spring.
So-kan   Double trunk which divides close to the base of the trunk.
Kabudachi   Multiple trunk – single tree at the base, splitting into several trunks to form a group.
Hokidachi   Broom style, the head is shaped like a broom.
Fukinagashi   Windswept style – all the branches lean in one direction.
Neagari   Exposed root system.
Netsuranari   Connecting-root style – an odd number of trees growing from the same root system.
Ishitsuki   Tree or trees grown on a rock.
Ikadabuki   Raft style – the trunk leans on its side and the branches are only allowed to develop on one side, giving the illusion of several trees growing in a clump.
Yose-ue   Group planting which resembles a forest.

Root pruning   Every two years for up to six years, then every two to three depending on the rate of growth.
Wiring   March.
Propagation   Cuttings – softwood and semi-ripe.
Pests   Mainly trouble-free.
Diseases   Die-back and yellow leaves. Keep movement of the tree to a minimum, give as much light as possible and remove from glass areas during frost periods. Never allow the compost to become too dry.

Sophora japonica (Japanese pagoda tree)

Originating from China and Korea, this cold-room flowering bonsai bears white, pea-like flowers, followed by long pods containing the seed.

Compost   Code 4.
Position   Plenty of light and sun, good ventilation, can be kept outside in a south-facing position during a warm summer, but sheltered from strong winds.
Temperature   Winter: 10°C (50°F). Summer: between 16–18°C (61–64°F).

Styles for the Japanese Pagoda Tree

Chokkan   Formal upright or straight-trunk style.
Moyogi   Curving or informal upright trunk.
Shakan   Leaning or slanting trunk.
Bankan   Twisted trunk, coiled almost like a spring.
So-kan   Double trunk which divides close to the base of the trunk.
Kabudachi   Multiple trunk – single tree at the base, splitting into several trunks to form a group.
Hokidachi   Broom style, the head or foliage is shaped like a broom.
Fukinagashi   Windswept style – all the branches lean in one direction.
Neagari   Exposed root system.
Ishitsuki   Tree or trees grown on a rock.

Watering   Summer: every day; winter: every two to three days.
Root pruning   Every year for up to five years, then every two.
Wiring   March.
Propagation   Seed: sow during the months of March and April in compost Code 1. If kept in a coldframe or glasshouse, no heat is required.
Pests   Mainly trouble-free.
Diseases   Mainly trouble-free.

Sophora microphylla (kowhai)

Originates from New Zealand, smaller in height than *Sophora tetraptera*. Bears same-coloured flower in April and May, followed by long pods containing seed.

Chinese water elm. Fares better if kept in a cold room.

Styles for the Kowhai

Chokkan   Formal upright or straight-trunk style.
Moyogi   Curving or informal upright trunk.
Shakan   Leaning or slanting trunk.
Bankan   Twisted trunk, coiled almost like a spring.
So-kan   Double trunk which divides close to the base of the trunk.
Kabudachi   Multiple trunk – single tree at the base, splitting into several trunks to form a group.
Hokidachi   Broom style, the head or foliage is shaped like a broom.
Fukinagashi   Windswept style – all the branches lean in one direction.
Neagari   Exposed root system.
Ishitsuki   Tree or trees grown on a rock.

Styles for the Chinese Water Elm

Chokkan   Formal upright or straight-trunk style.
Moyogi   Curving or informal upright trunk.
Shakan   Leaning or slanting trunk.
Bankan   Twisted trunk, coiled almost like a spring.
So-kan   Double trunk which divides close to the base of the trunk.
Kabudachi   Multiple trunk – single tree at the base, splitting into several trunks to form a group.
Hokidachi   Broom style, the head or foliage is shaped like a broom.
Fukinagashi   Windswept style – all the branches lean in one direction.
Neagari   Exposed root system.
Netsuranari   Connecting-root style – an odd number of trees growing from the same root system.
Ishitsuki   Tree or trees grown on a rock.
Ikadabuki   Raft style – the trunk leans on its side and the branches are only allowed to develop on one side, giving the illusion of several trees growing in a clump.
Yose-ue   Group planting which resembles a forest.

Compost   Code 4.
Position   Plenty of light and sun, good ventilation, place outside in a south-facing position during warm days in the summer, but out of cold winds.
Temperature   Winter: 10°C (50°F). Summer: between 16–18°C (61–64°F).
Watering   Summer: every day; winter: every three days.

Root pruning Every year for up to five years, then every two.
Wiring March.
Propagation Seed: sow during the months of March and April in compost Code 1. Place in a cold frame or glasshouse (no heat is required).
Pests Mainly trouble-free.
Diseases Mainly trouble-free.

Sophora tetraptera (kowhai)

Originates from New Zealand. It may also be called the New Zealand laburnum. Good cold-room, flowering bonsai for the beginner. The flowers are yellow, followed by long pods.

Ulmus parviflora (Chinese water elm)

Semi-evergreen cold-room bonsai. Small thick trunk in a short space of time. More tree-like than most other indoor bonsai.

Compost Code 4.
Position Place in a cool position with plenty of light. Place outside from mid-May to September, avoid frost.
Temperature Summer: between 10–22°C (50–72°F). Winter: do not allow to drop below 6°C (43°F).
Watering Summer: every day; winter: every two to three days.
Root pruning Every year for up to five years, then every two to three depending on the rate of growth.
Wiring March and August.
Propagation Seed or cuttings – softwood or semi-ripe.
Pests Mainly trouble-free.
Diseases Mainly trouble-free.

GLOSSARY

JAPANESE TERMS

Bankan Twisting trunk, coiled almost like a spring.

Bunjingi Known as *Literati* style; long bare trunk with top growth.

Chokkan Formal upright or straight-trunk style.

Fukinagashi Windswept style – all the branches lean in the same direction.

Go-kan Five trunks.

Han-kengai Semi-cascade tree; cascades more to a 45° angle.

Hokidachi Broom style – often associated with the zelkova.

Ichi-no-eda The first branch on the tree.

Ikadabuki Raft style – the trunk is placed on its side, all upward-facing branches are then trained as individual trees.

Ishitsuki Rock-grown style, tree or trees growing over rock.

Jin Withered and peeled branches, sometimes bleached white.

Jukei *'Jukei'* means 'style'.

Jushin Apex or top of tree.

Kabudachi Multiple-trunk style.

Katanebari A root which is one-sided.

Kengai A cascading tree.

Kuitsuki-eda A branch that is clinging.

Moyogi Curving or informal upright; one of the most popular styles used in bonsai.

Neagari Exposed root system, sometimes standing high above the soil surface.

Nebari The swelling of a root.

Netsuranari Root or roots that are connected.

Ni-no-eda The second branch of the tree.

Ochi-eda A drooping branch.

Omote The front of the tree.

Sabamiki A withered, peeled trunk.

San-kan Triple trunk.

San-no-eda The third branch on the tree.

Sashi-eda The largest branch on the tree.

Shakan Slanting-tree style.

Sharimiki Withered, peeled trunk.

Shihoo-nebari Roots which are growing in every direction.

So-kan The trunk splits into two just above soil-level.

Tachiagari The lower part of the trunk.

Tankan Single trunk.

Uke-eda A counterbalancing branch.

Ura The back of the tree.

Yaku-eda The essential branch of the tree.

Yose-ue Group plantings.

INDEX OF TREE NAMES

Acacia, 148
Acer (maple), 110
Adansonia (baobab), 149
Aesculus (horse chestnut), 113
Alnus (alder), 115
Amelanchier (snowy mespilus), 117
Araucaria araucana, 150
Arbutus (strawberry tree), 117
Arundinaria (bamboo), 117
Azalea, 142

Bambusa multiplex (bamboo), 150
Betula (silver birch), 118
Brachychiton (bottle tree), 151
Buxus (box), 120

Callicarpa, 121
Carmona, 151
Carpinus (hornbeam), 122
Casuarina (beefwood tree), 152
Catalpa (Indian bean tree), 124
Cedrus (cedar), 124
Celastrus (bittersweet), 125
Ceratonia (carob), 152
Cercis (Judas tree), 125
Chaenomeles (Japanese quince), 126
Chamaecyparis (false cypress), 126
Chamaedorea (palm), 153
Citrus, 153
Cornus (dogwood), 126
Cotoneaster, 127
Crassula (jade tree), 156
Crataegus (hawthorn), 128
Cryptomeria (Japanese cedar), 129
Cycas (sago palm), 156

Dracaena (dragon tree), 157

Elaeagnus, 129
Erythrina (coral tree), 157

Eucalyptus, 158
Euonymus (spindle tree), 130

Fagus (beech), 130
Ficus, 160
Forsythia, 131
Fraxinus (ash), 132
Fuschia, 133

Gardenia, 160
Gleditsia, 133

Ilex (holly), 134

Jasminum (winter flowering jasmine), 134
Juniperus (juniper), 135

Laburnum (golden rain), 135
Lagerstroemia (Chinese crape myrtle), 161
Larix (larch), 135
Lonicera (honeysuckle), 136

Malpighia (Barbados cherry), 161
Malus (flowering crab apple), 136
Metrosideros (Christmas torch), 162
Morus (mulberries), 137
Murraya (jasmine orange), 162
Musa (banana), 162
Myrtus (myrtle), 163

Nandina (Chinese sacred bamboo), 163
Nothofagus (beech), 138

Olea (olive), 164

Patanga (Malayan apple), 165
Phoenix (date palm), 165
Picea (spruce), 138

Pinus (Jerusalem pine), 166
Pinus densiflora (Japanese red pine), 92
Pinus parviflora (Japanese white pine), 93
Pinus thunbergii (Japanese black pine), 93
Pistacia (pistachio), 167
Populus (poplar), 139
Prunus (flowering cherry), 139
Punica (pomegranate), 167
Pyracantha (firethorn), 141

Quercus (oak), 141

Rhododendron arboreum (rhododendron), 142
Robinia (common acacia), 142

Sageretia, 169
Salix (willow), 142
Sequoia, 143
Serissa (tree of a thousand stars), 169
Sophora japonica (Japanese pagoda tree), 170
Sophora microphylla (kowhai), 171
Sorbus, 144
Stewartia (stuartia), 144
Sucmus (Chinese water elm), 172

Tamarix (tamarisk), 145
Taxus (yew), 145
Tsuga (hemlock), 145

Ulmus (elm), 146
Ulmus parviflora (Chinese water elm), 172

Wisteria, 146

Zelkova (grey bark elm), 146

GENERAL INDEX

air layering, 56
aphids, 64

base exchange, 31
bone meal, 41
bonsai names and styles,
    29
botrytis, 45
buds/budding, 89

calcium, 38
canker, 70
capillary action, 34
capsid bugs, 66
carbon, 37
caterpillars, 66
cells, 39
chemicals, 63
chlorosis, 38
clay, 31
cold frame, 53
compost, 34
compost mixing, 36
coral spot, 70
cultivated trees, 85
cuttings, 50
cuttings list, 55

damping off, 45
die back, 70
diseases, 70
drawing plan, 19
dried blood, 40
driftwood planting, 98

exposed roots, 87

FYM, 41
feeding, 12, 31
fish guano, 40
flaccid cell, 39
foliar feed, 38

frost, 61
fungicide, 45

gall mites, 67
galls, 71
grafting, 58
    roots, 88
    wax, 59
grey mould, 45
group plantings, 103

hardwood cuttings, 11, 51
hardy bonsai, 110
hoof and horn, 40
hydrogen, 37
hygiene, 63

imported trees, 10
indoor bonsai, 148
iron, 38

Jin, 98

landscapes, 106
layering, 56
leaf mould, 35, 92
leaf pruning, 89
light, 62
lime sulphur, 98
loam, 35

magnesium, 38
major elements, 37
manganese, 38
mealy bugs, 68
mist unit, 53
mites, 68
molybdenum, 38
multiple trunks, 105
mycorrhiza, 92

N.P.K., 37

natural grouping, 103
nitrogen, 37
non-organic compost, 36
nursery specimens, 85
nursery stock, 46

organic compost, 35
organic feed, 39
organic seed compost, 44
osmosis, 39
overfeeding, 38
oxygen, 37

pH, 32
peat, 35
pinching, 96
placement, 61
plants suitable for chalky soils,
    33
    for clay soils, 33
    for sandy soils, 33
plasmolysis, 39
potassium, 38
pots, 77
poultry manure, 41
propagation, 42
pruning, 64
    of pine, 95
    times, 17

raffia, 59
raft planting, 105
repotting, 19
rhododendron bugs, 68
rock plantings, 106
root over rock, 107
root pruning, 17

sand, 31
scale insects, 69
scorch, 12
seed collection, 42

seeds, 43
semi-ripe cuttings, 11, 51
silt, 31
softwood cuttings, 11, 51
soil, 30
sterilizing, 35
stock plant, 11
stratification, 43
sulphur, 38

temperature, 62
top growth, 103
trace elements, 38
training, 13
true groups, 104

unsuitable organic feeds, 41

warm bench, 53

watering, 12
weather conditions, 61
wild trees, 83
wild seeds, 42
wind, 63
wiring, 15
wood ash, 40

Zinc, 38